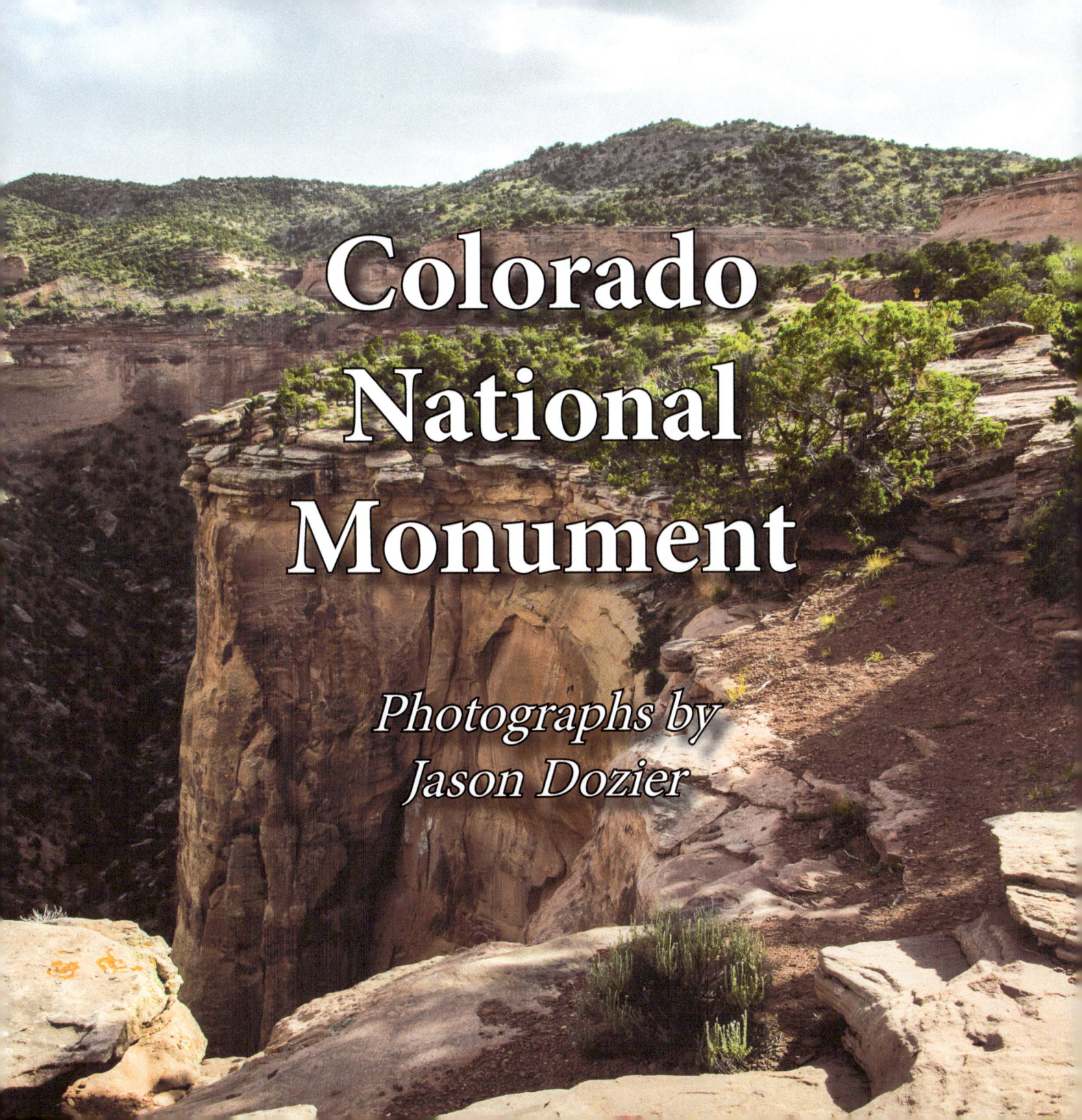

Colorado National Monument

Photographs by
Jason Dozier

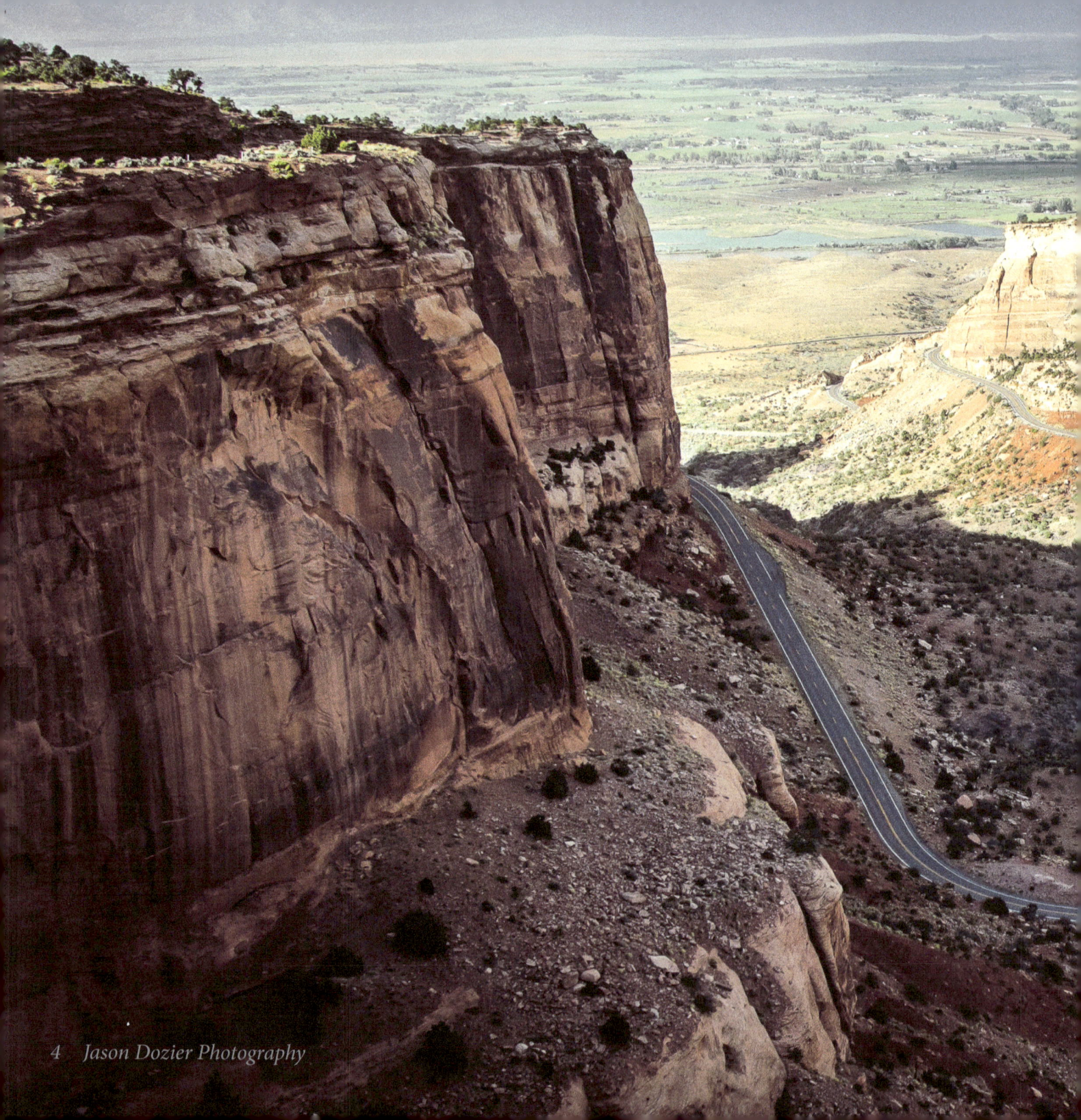

Jason Dozier Photography

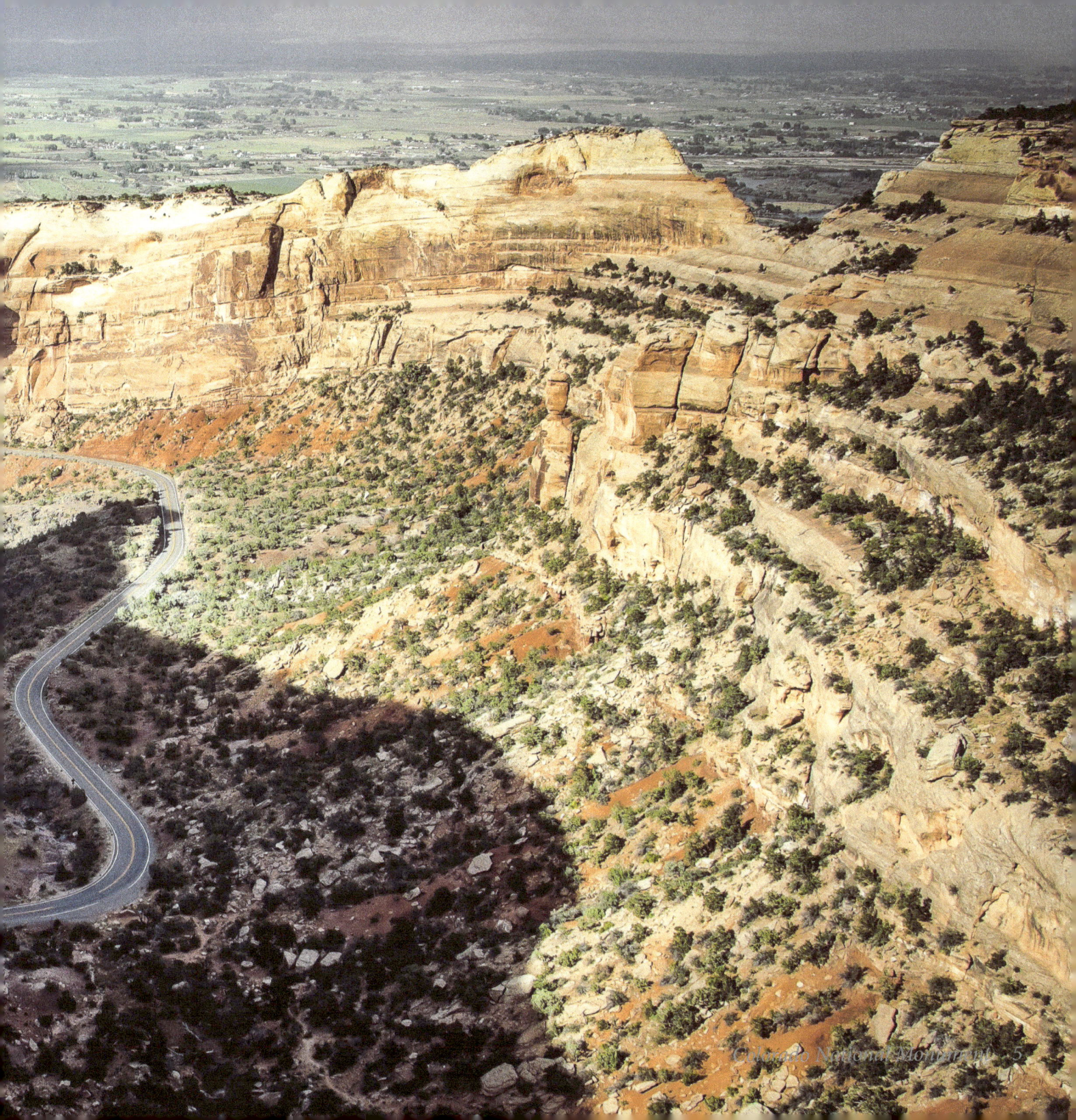

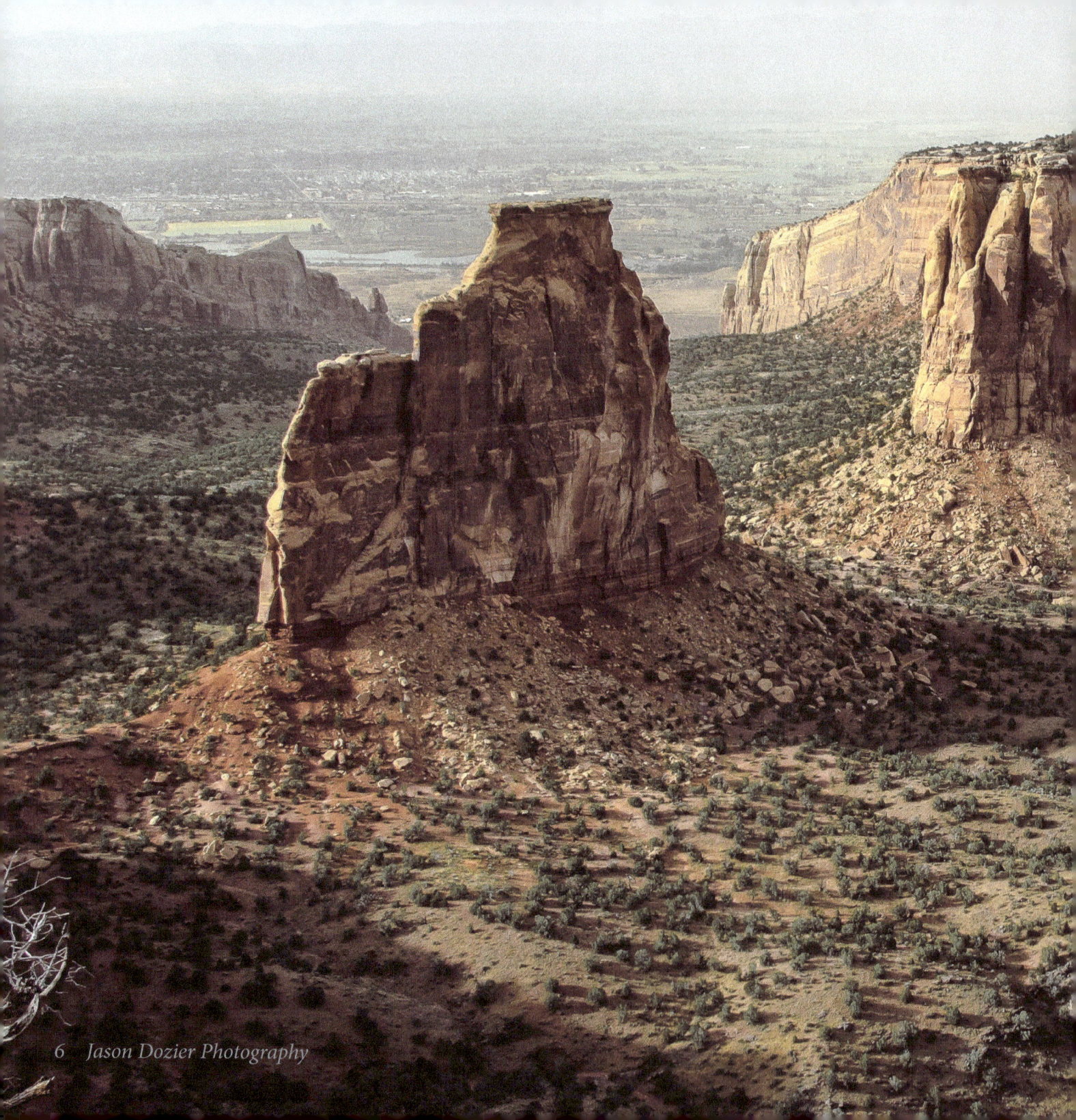

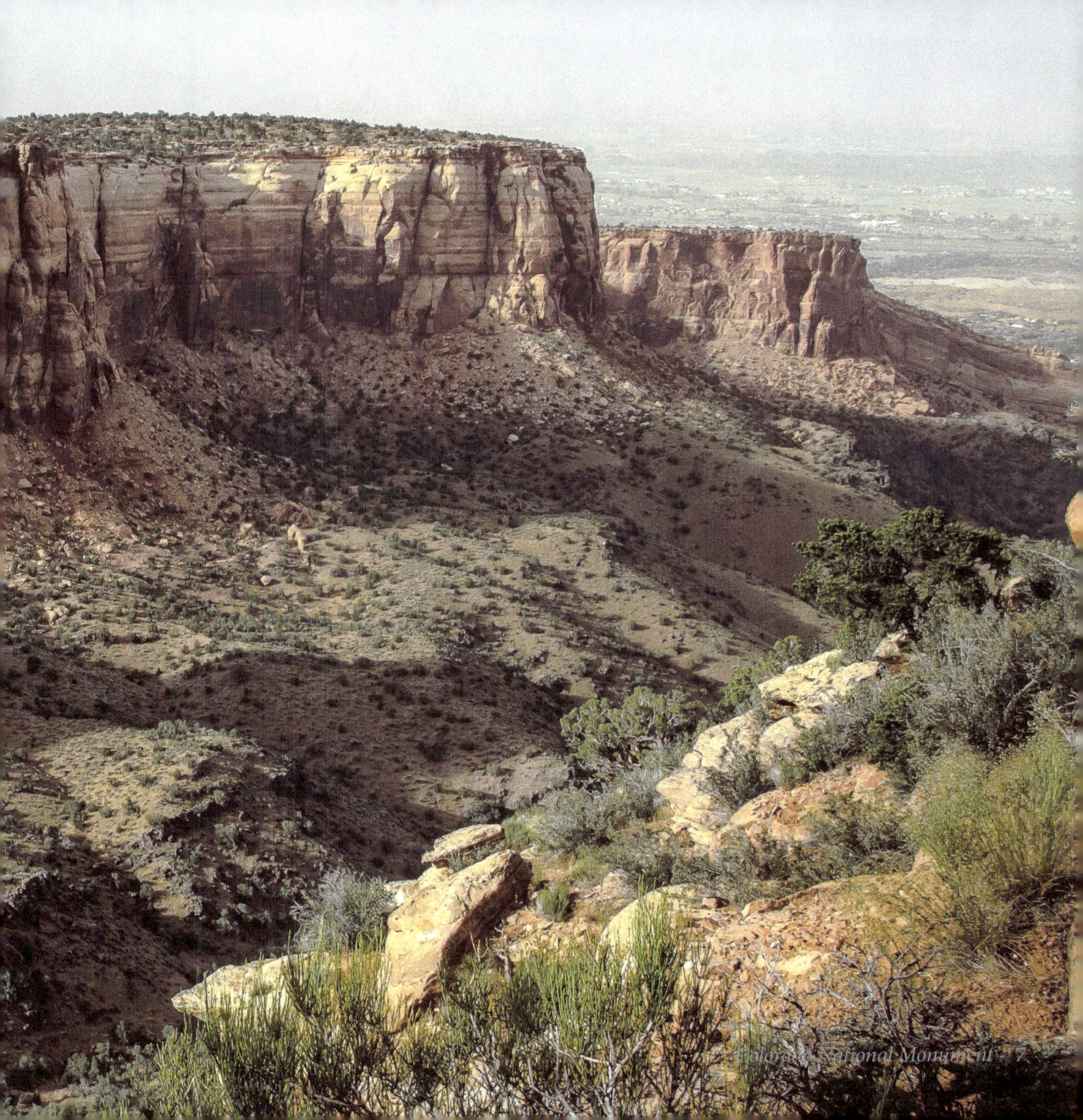

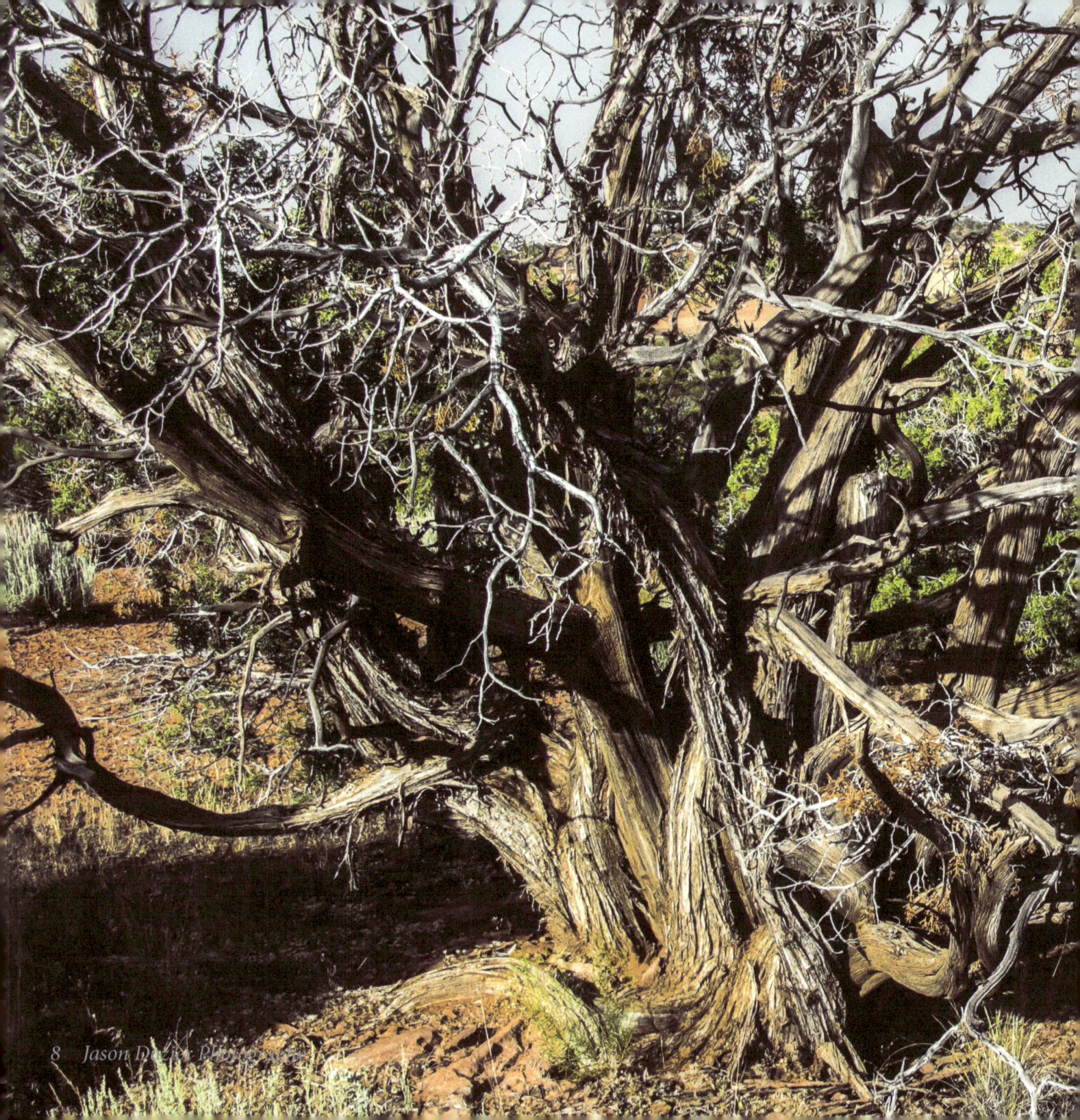

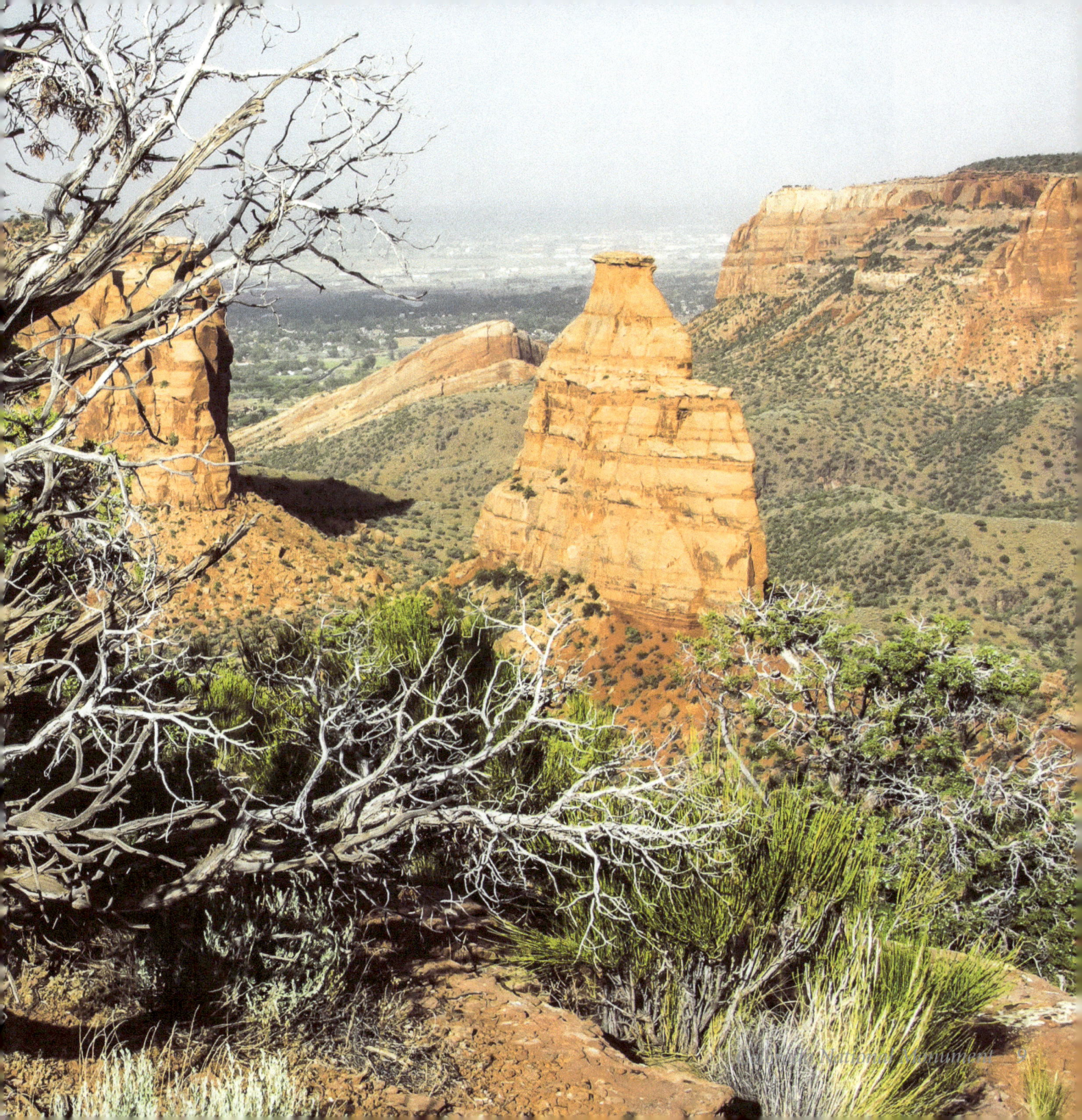

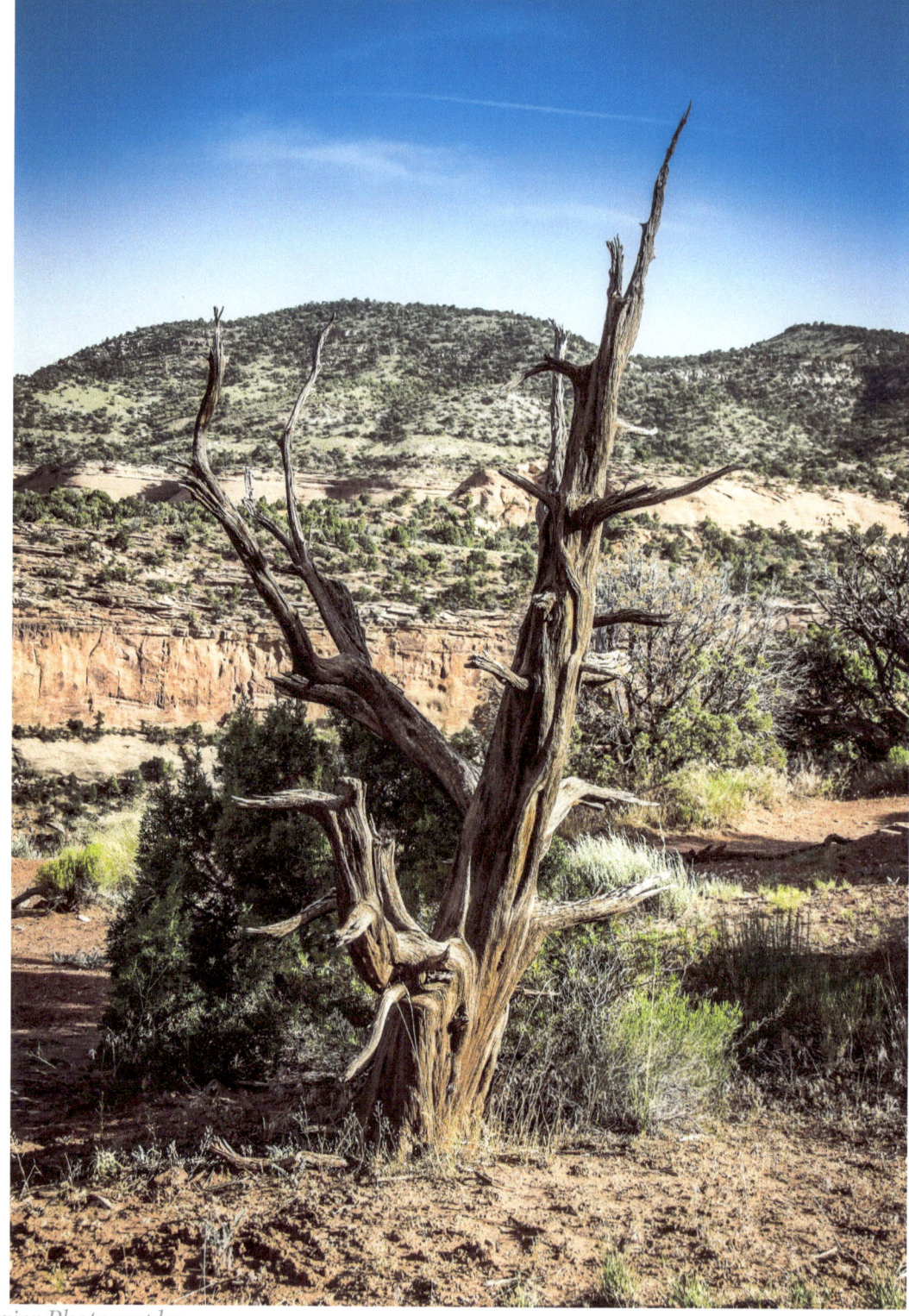

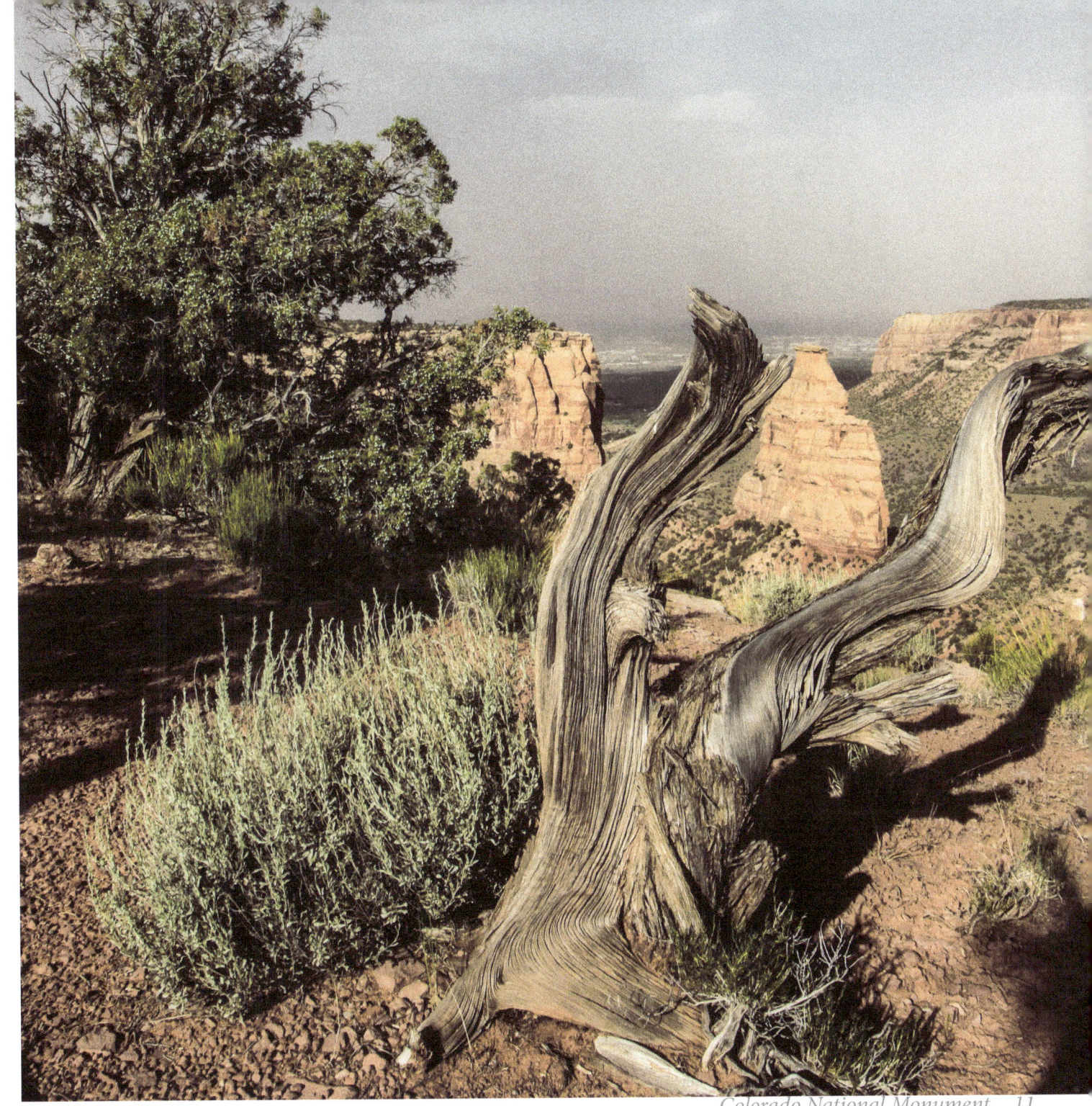

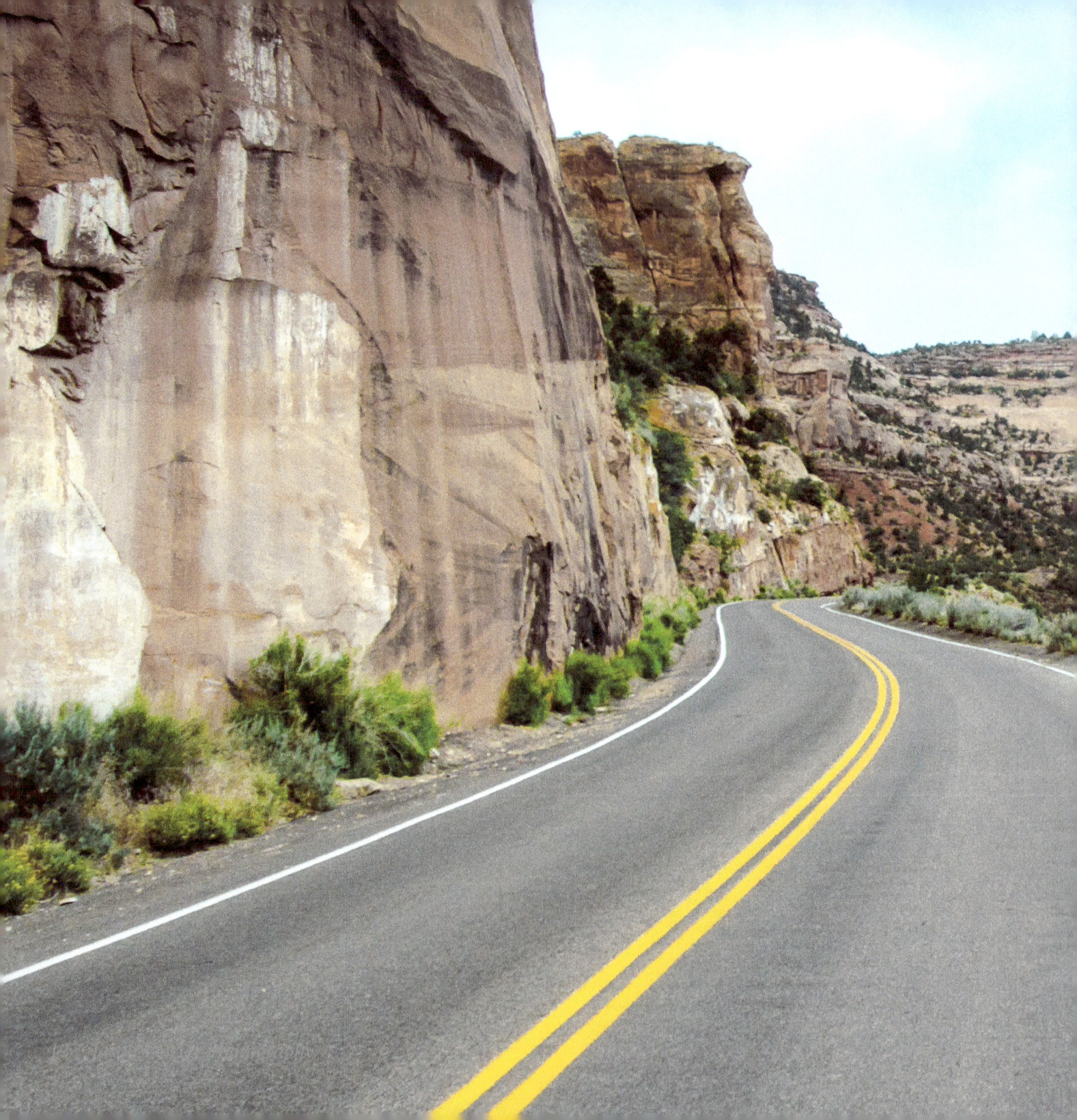

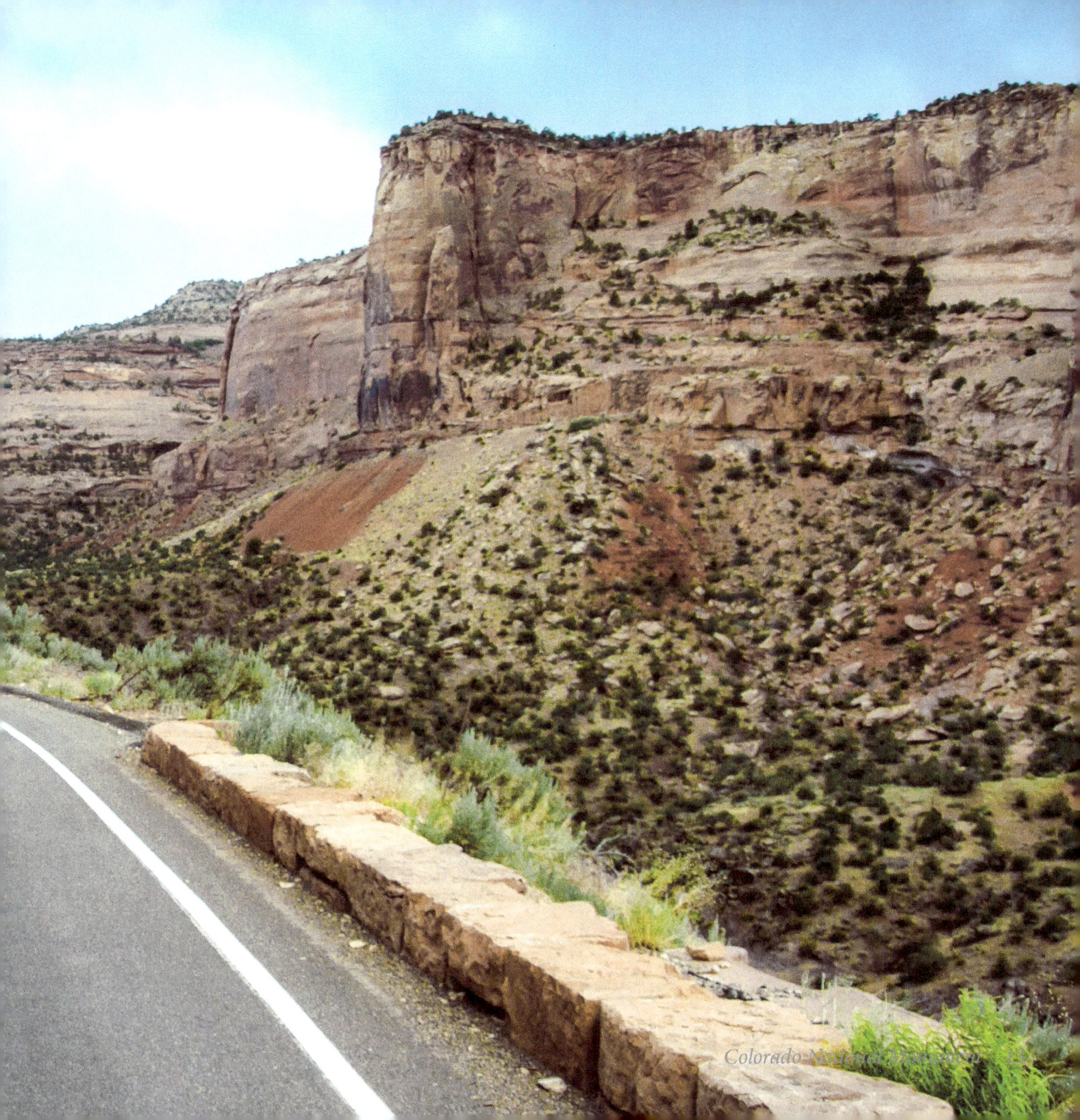

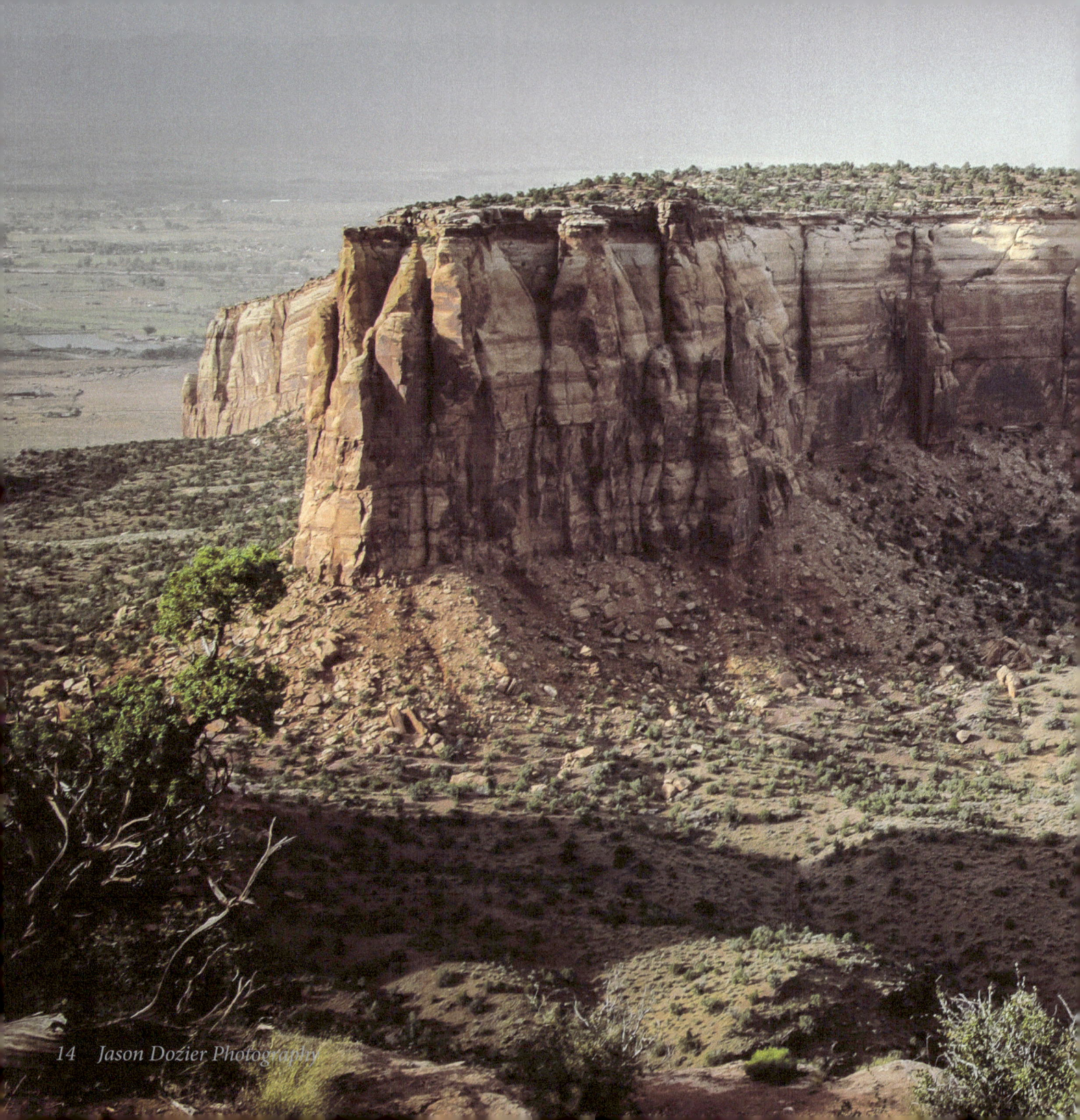

Jason Dozier Photography

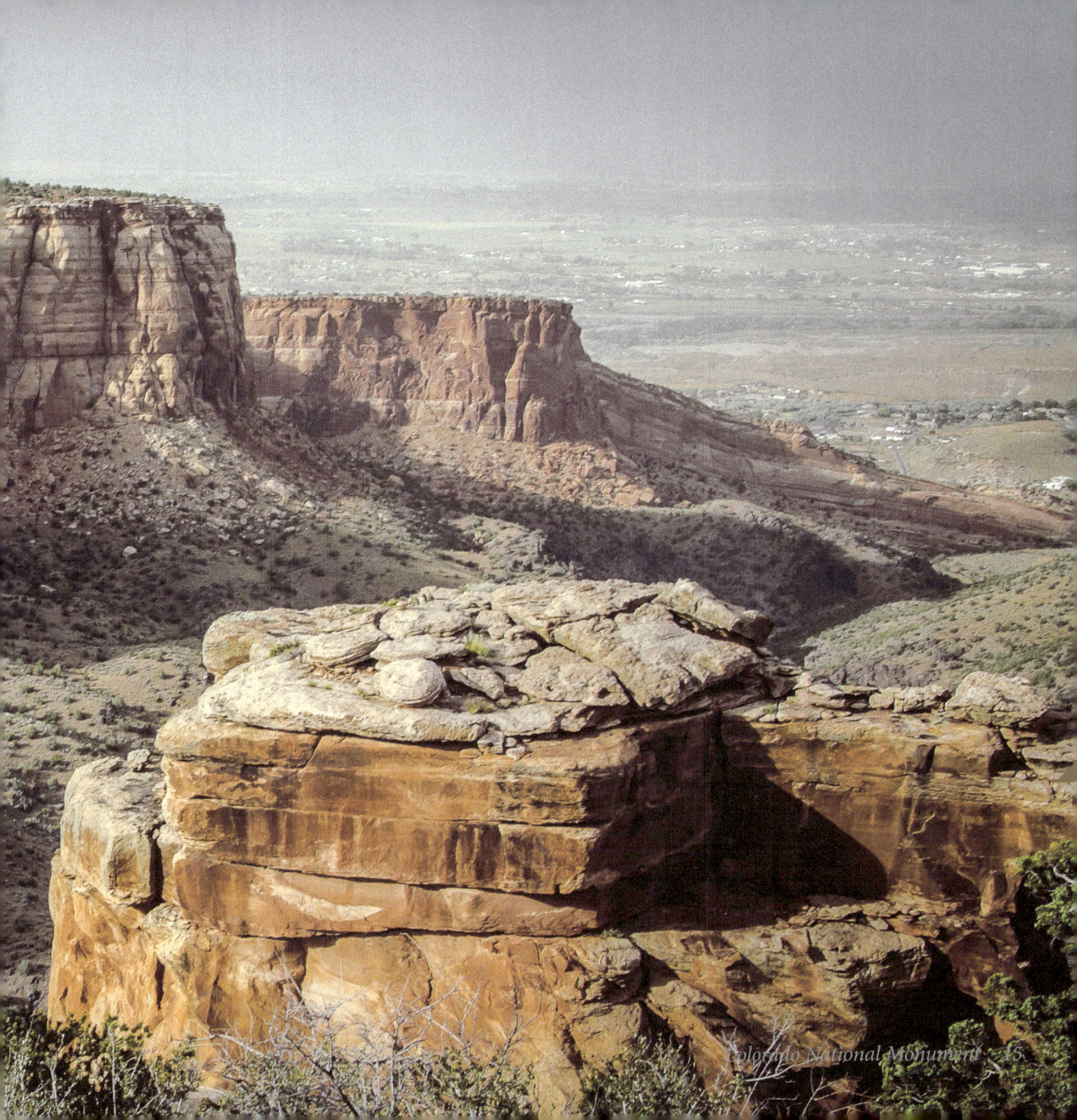

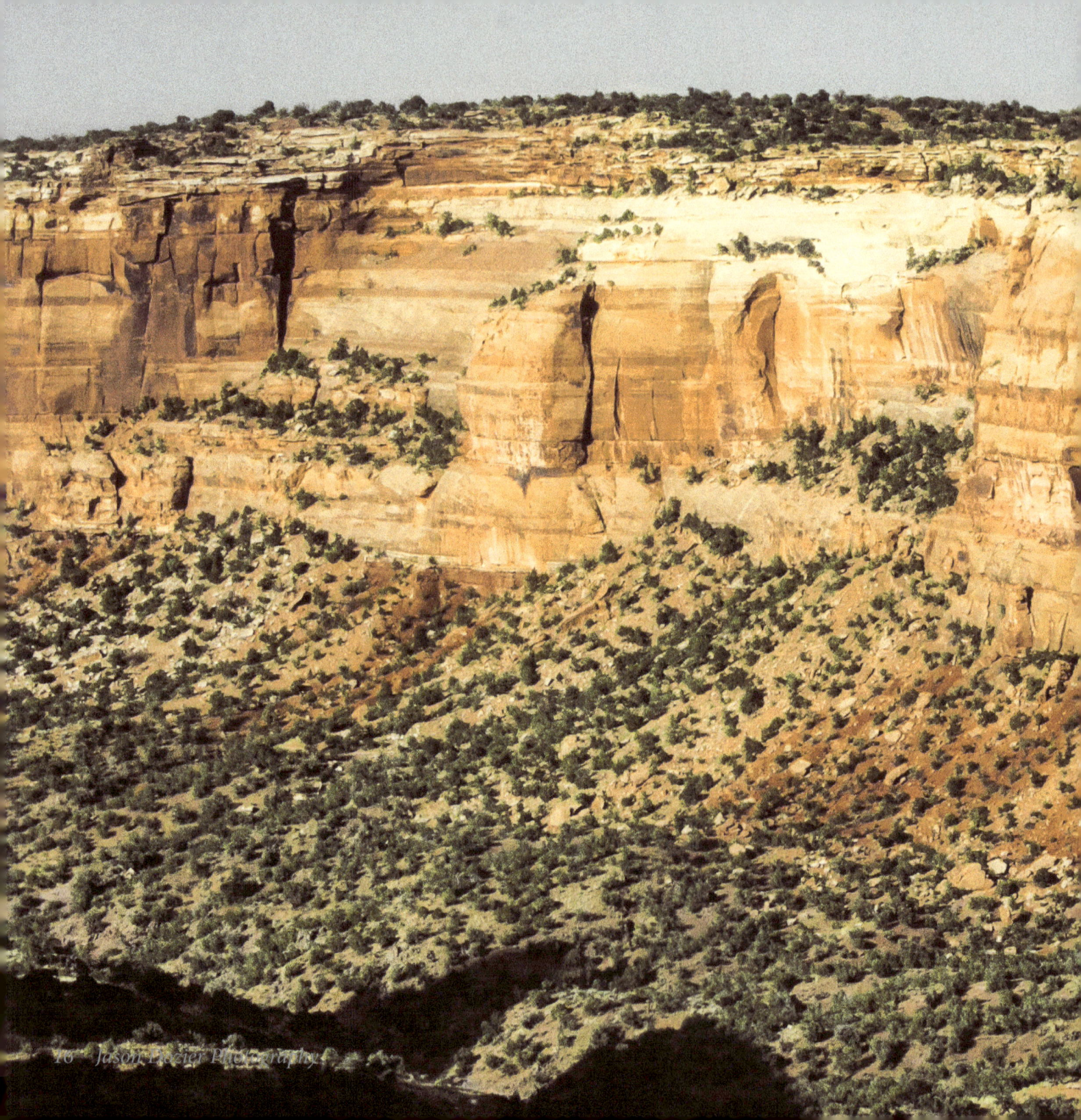

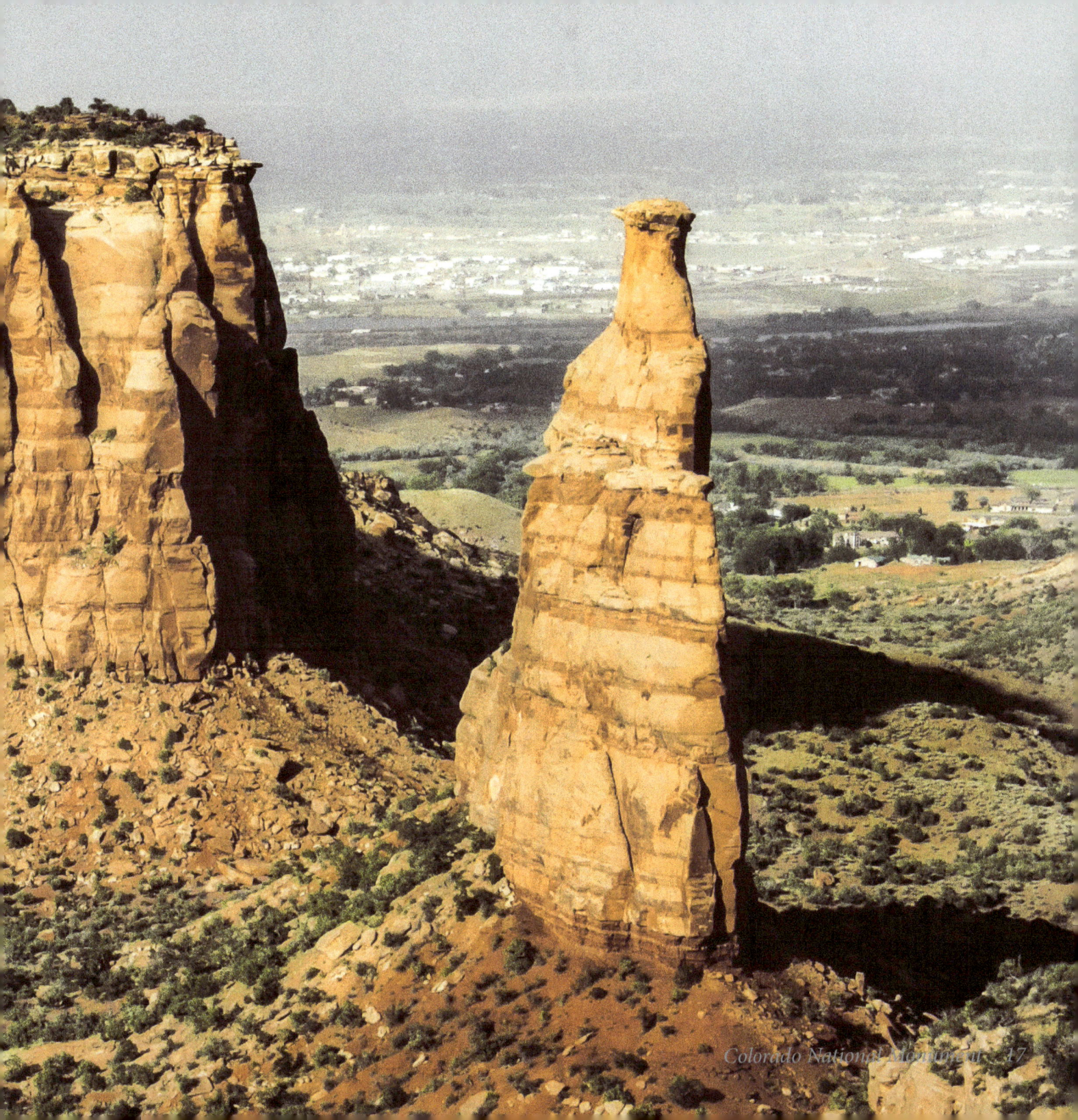

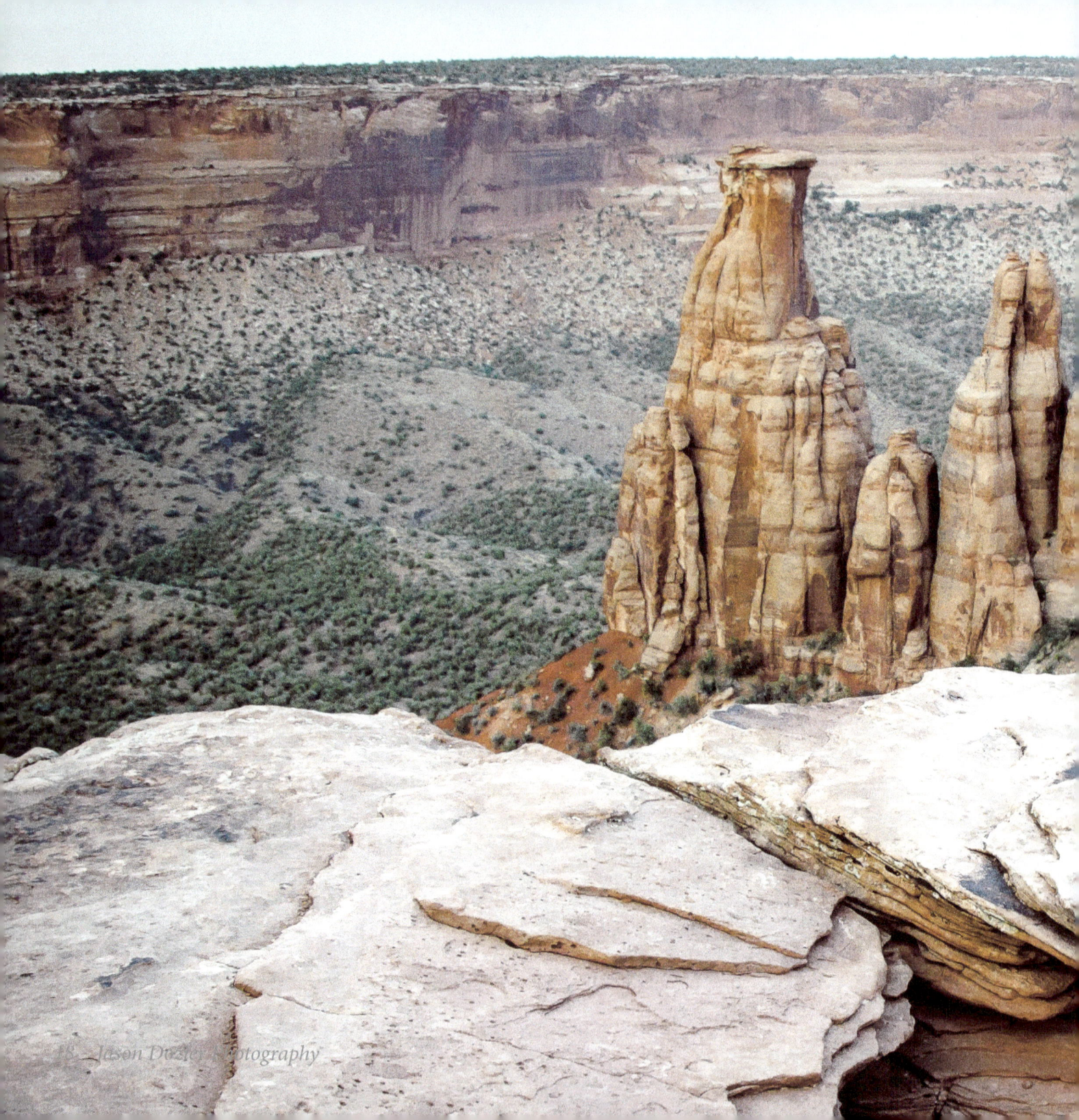

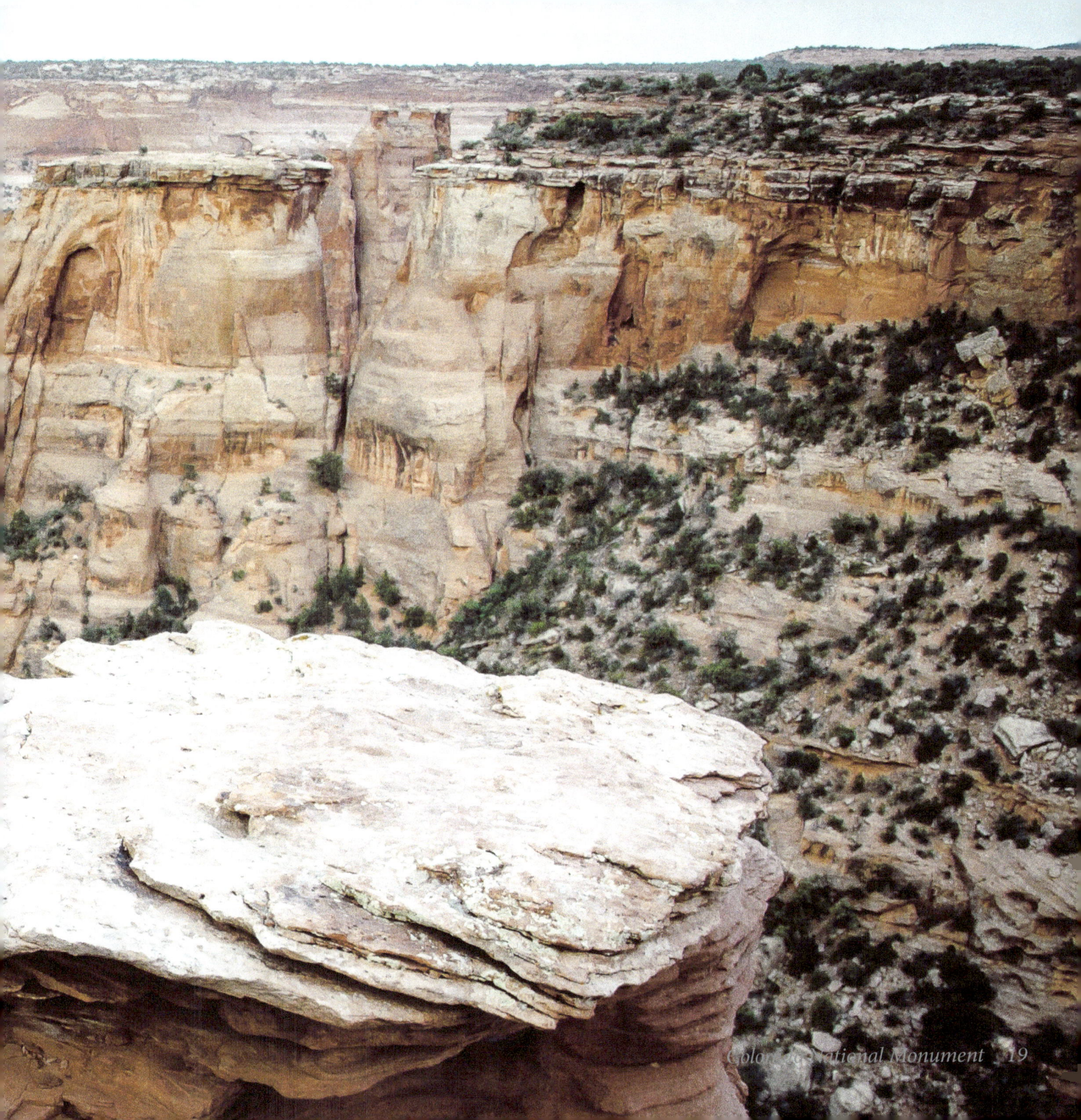

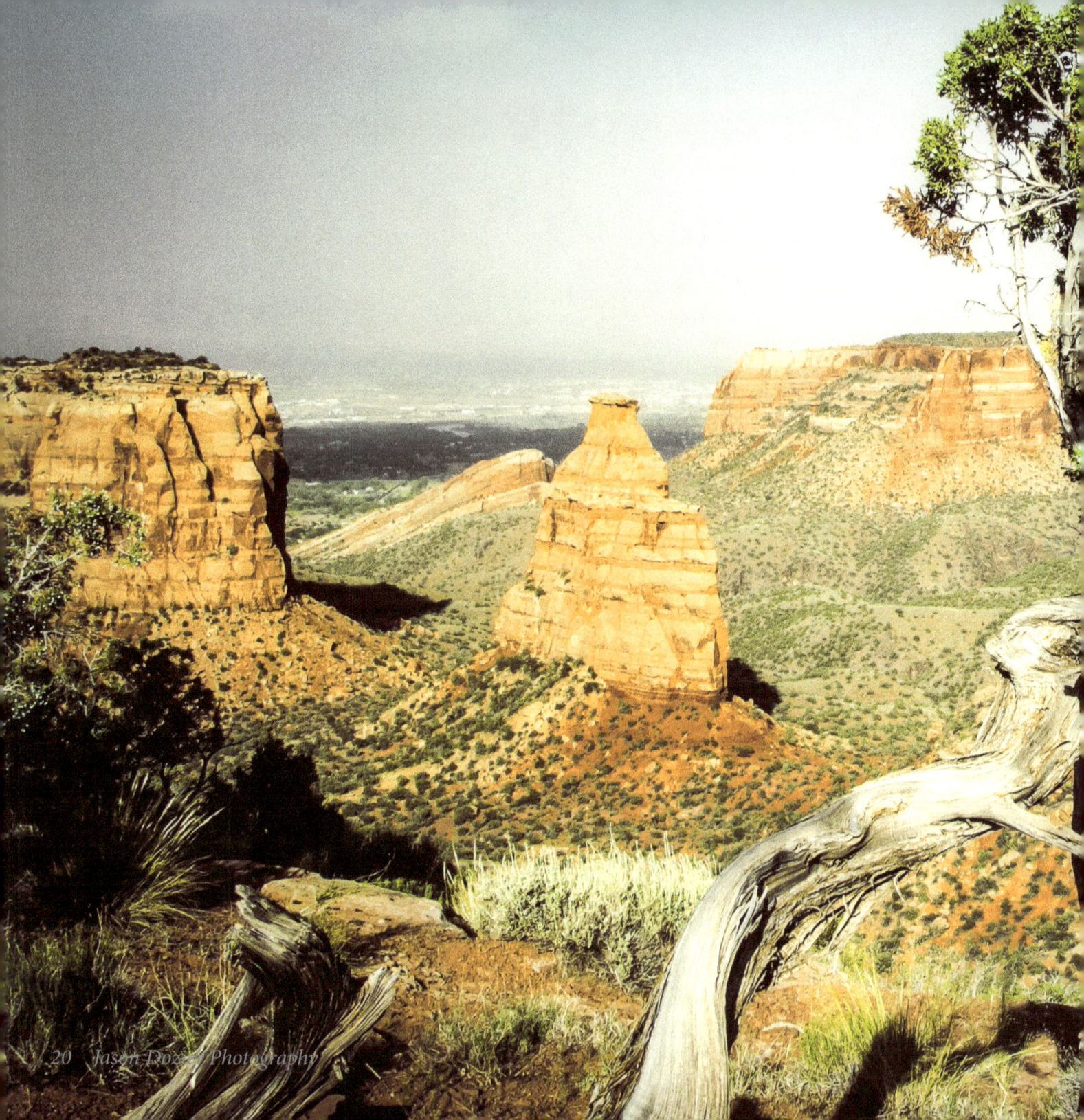

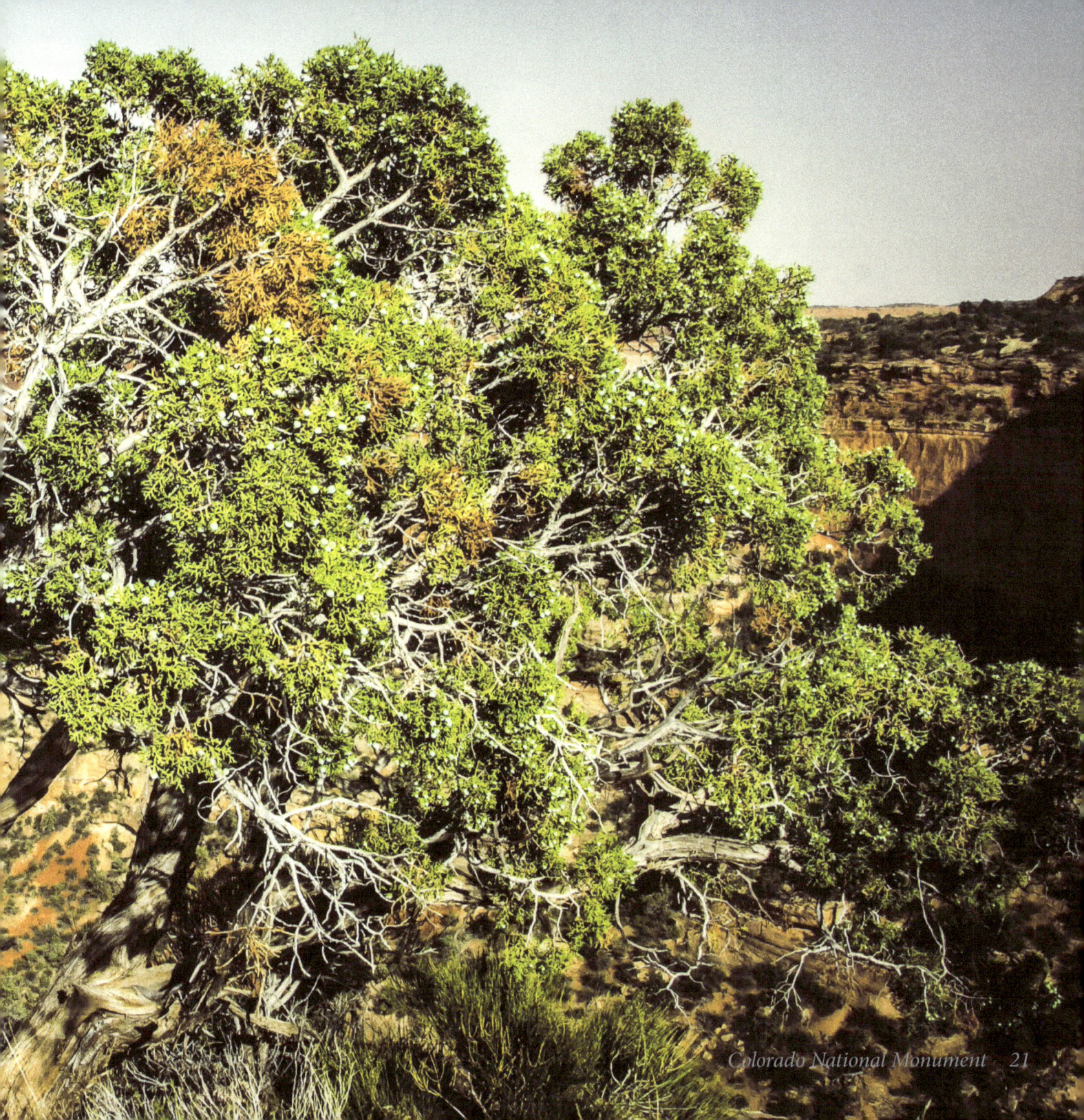

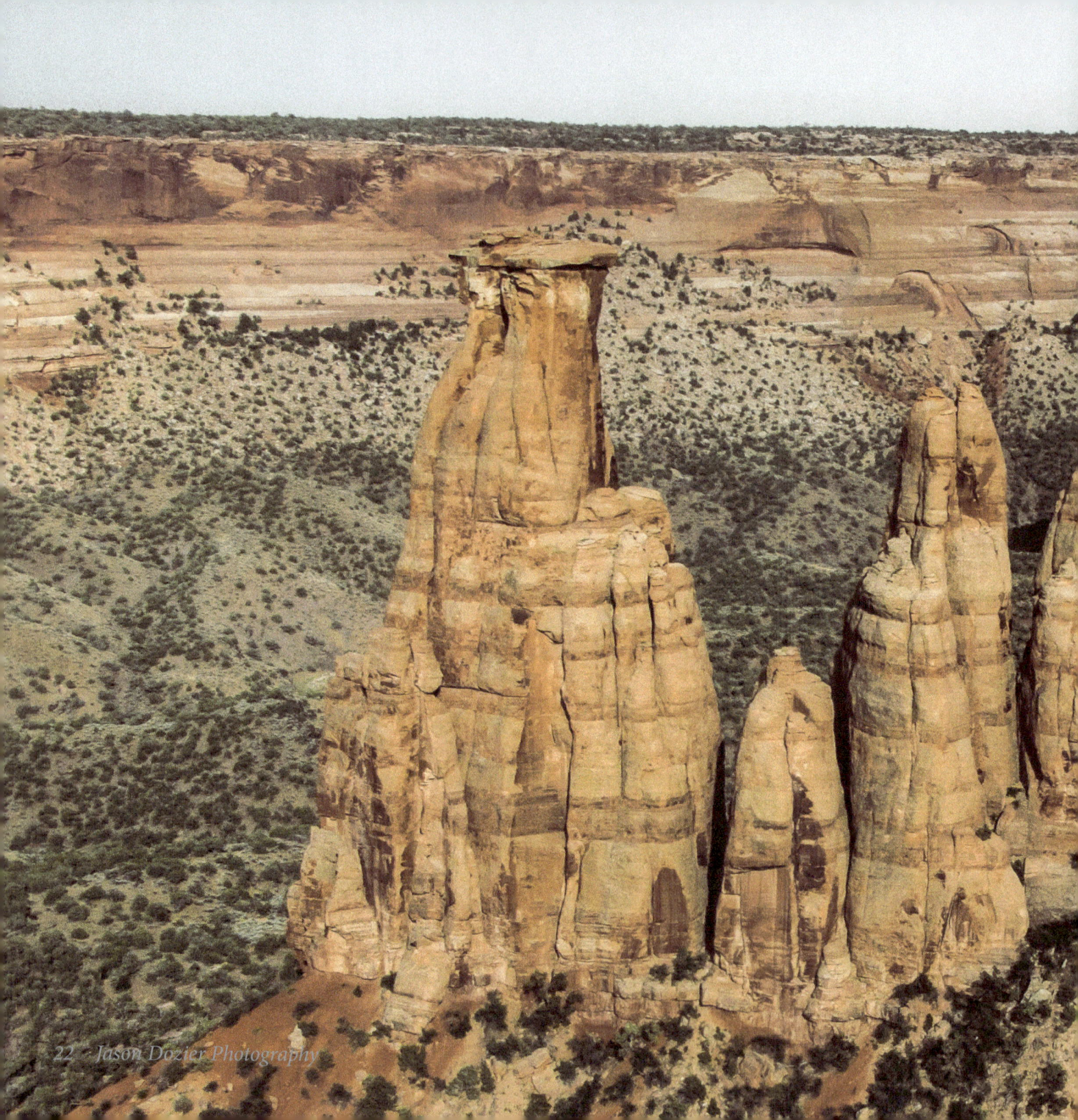

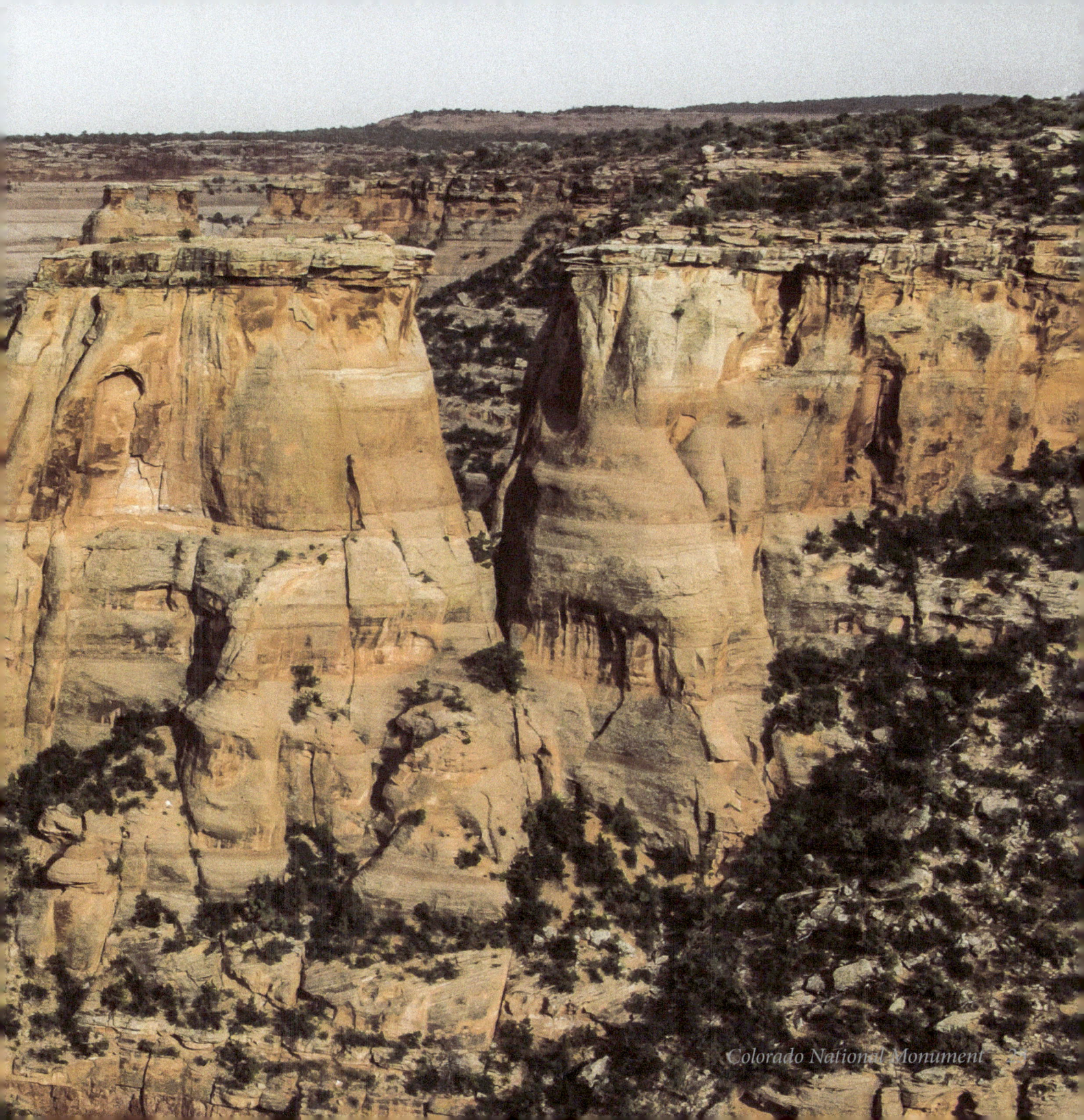

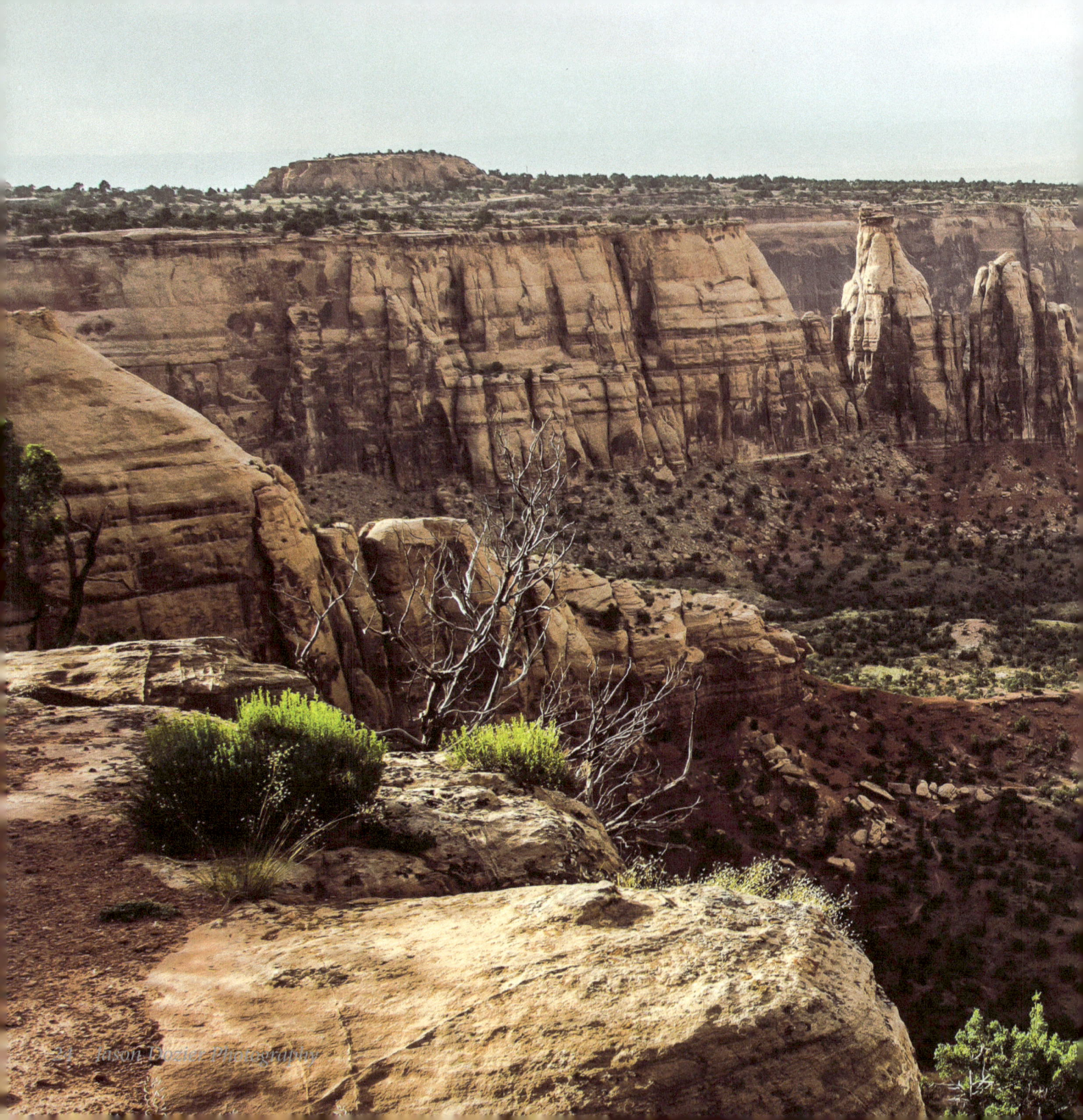

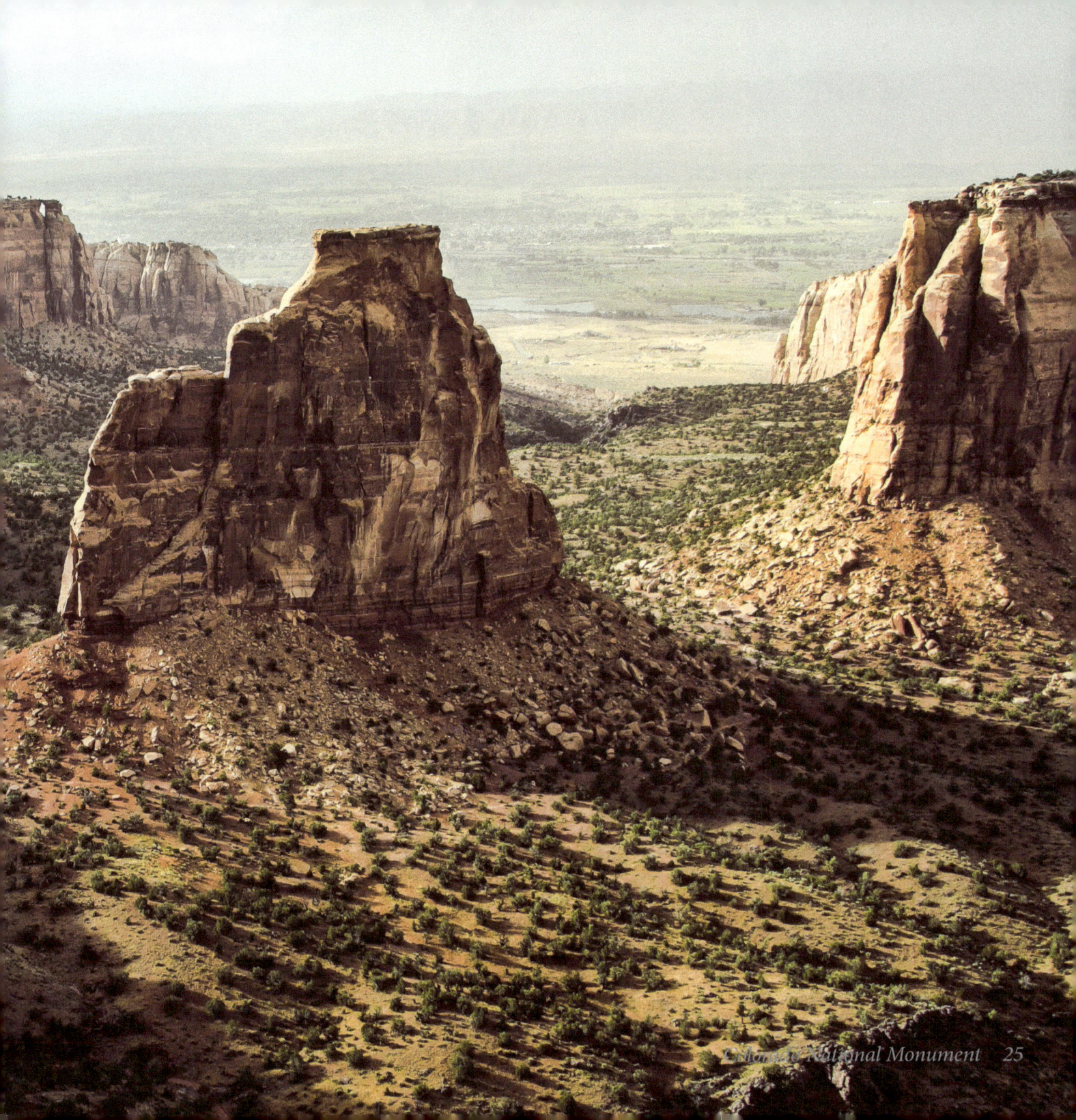

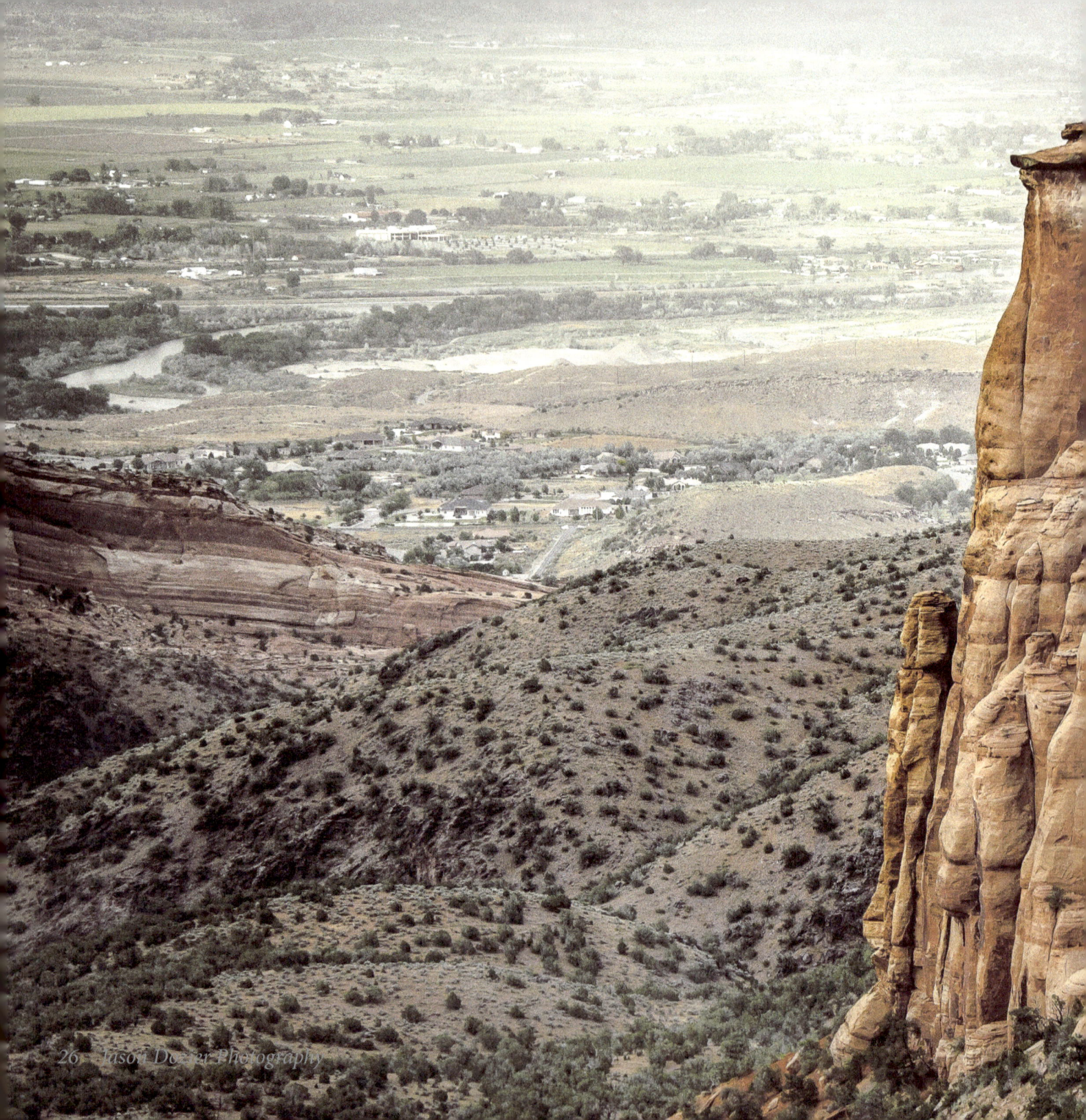

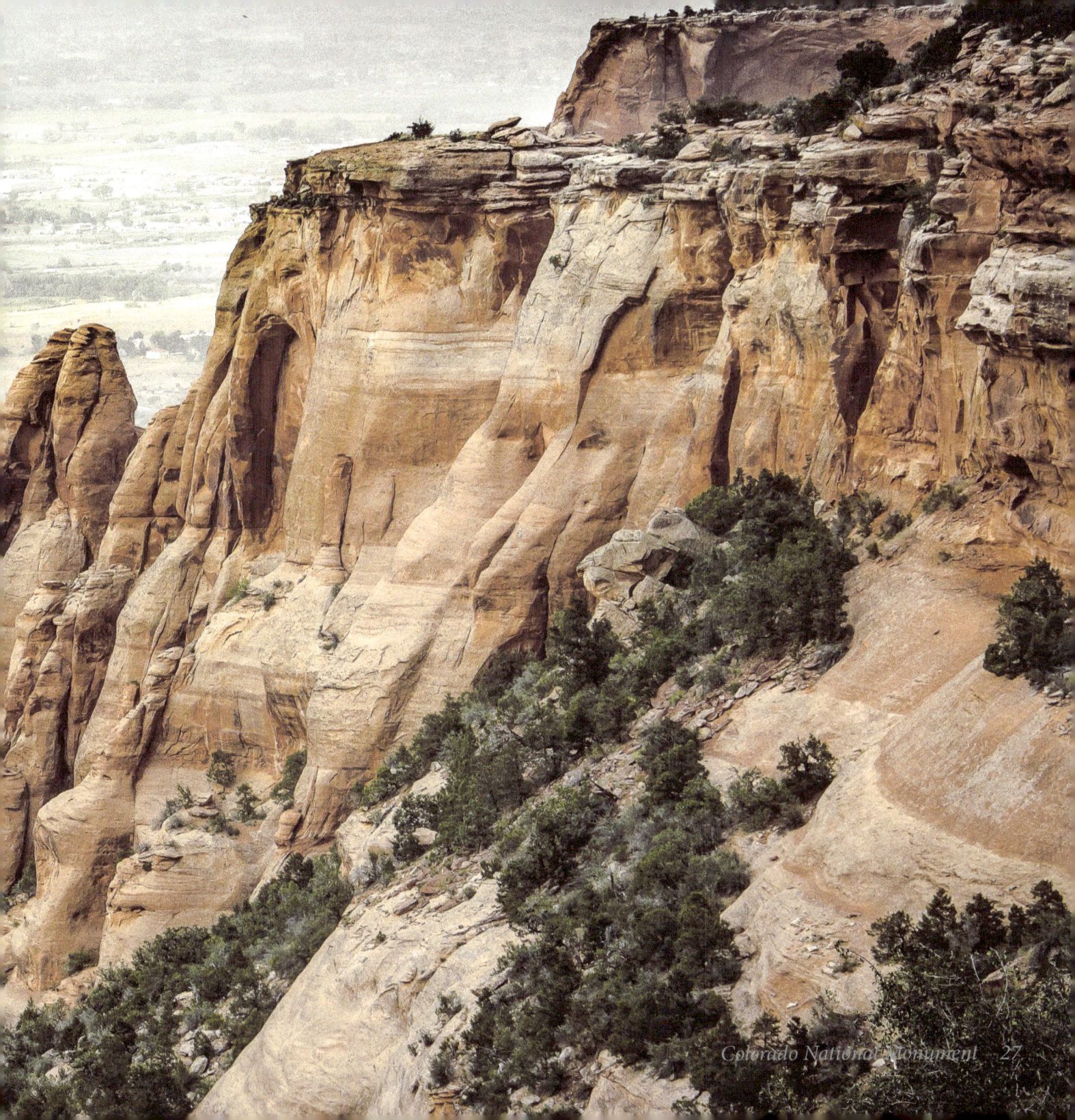

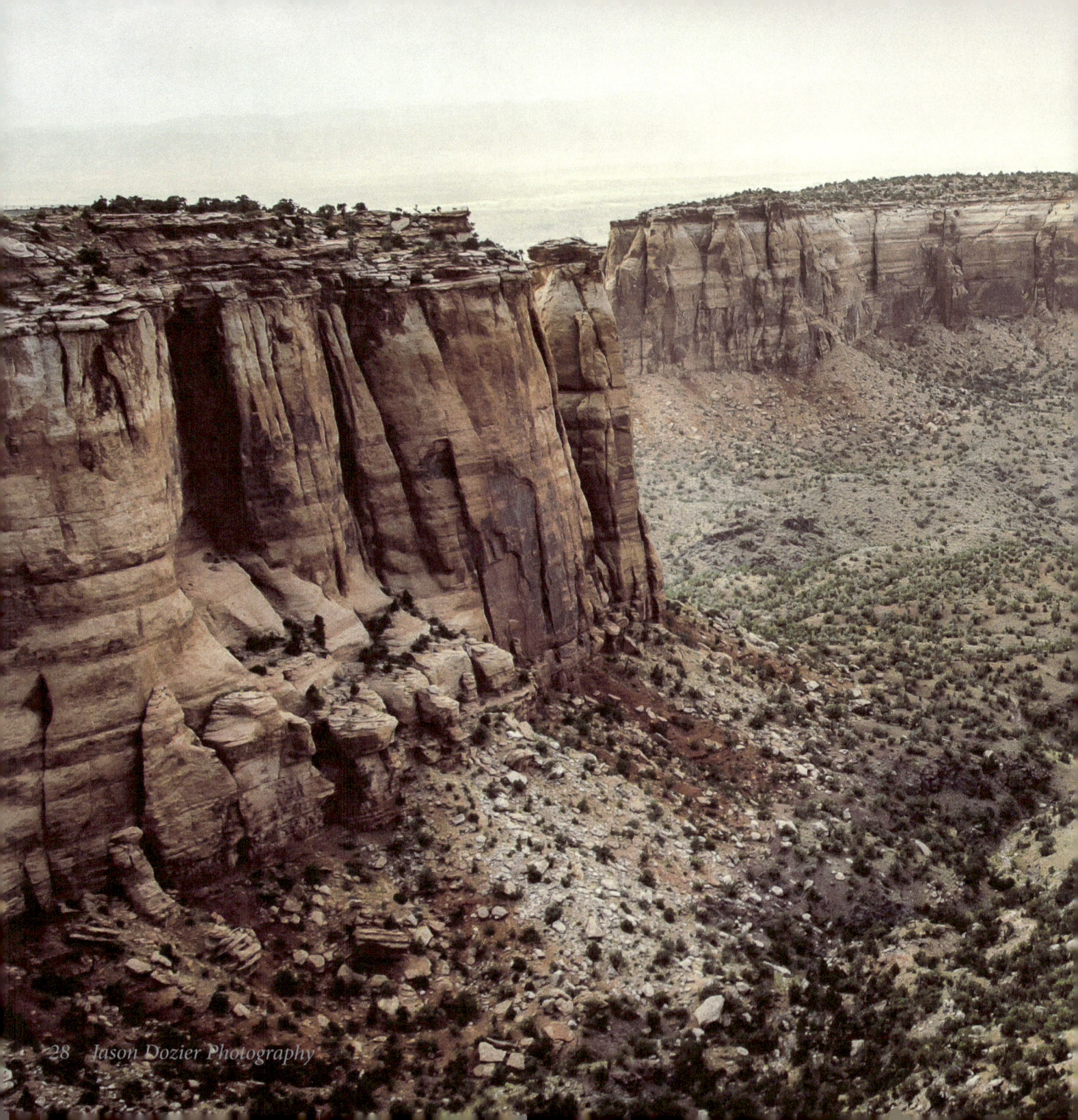

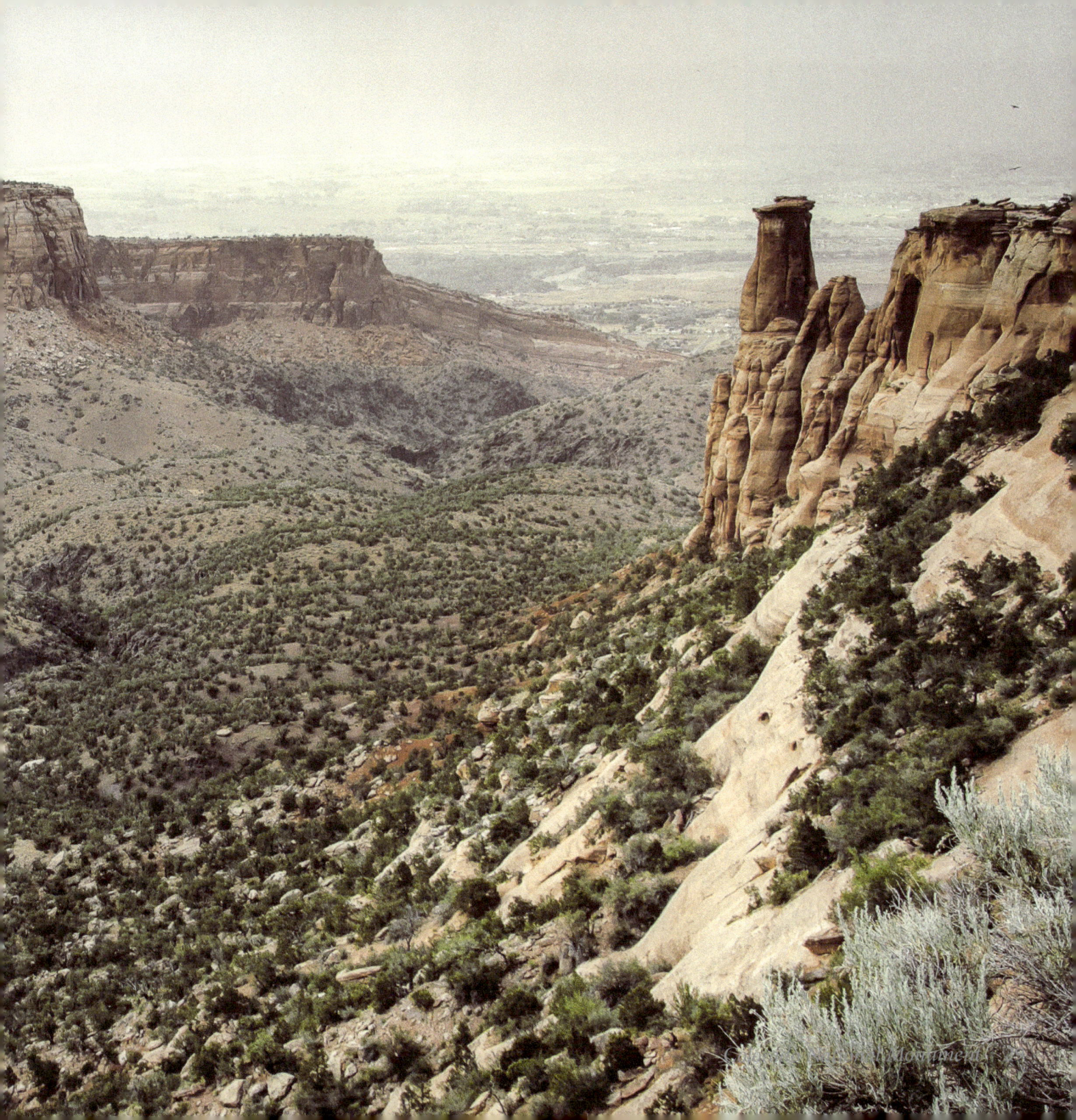

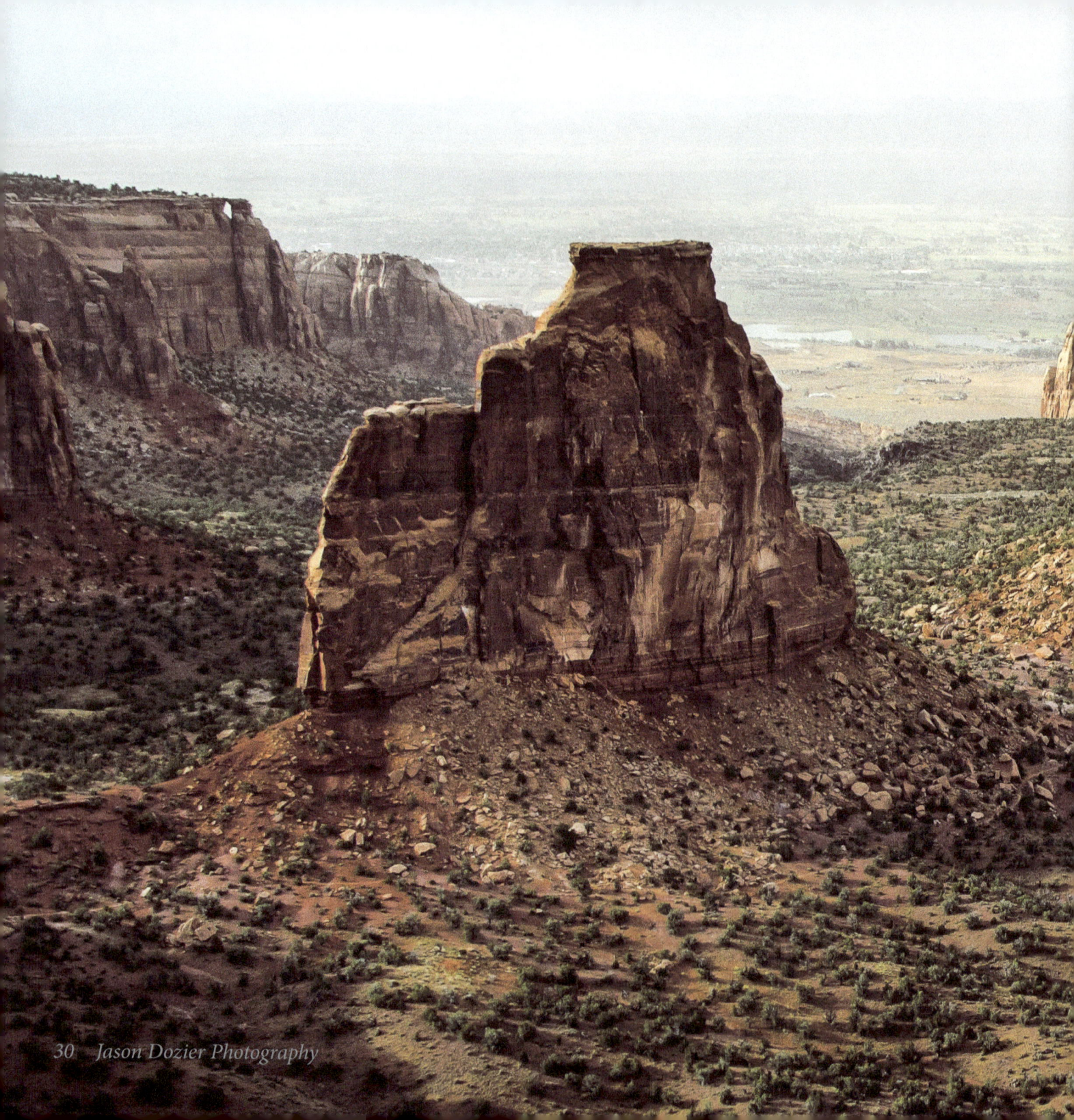

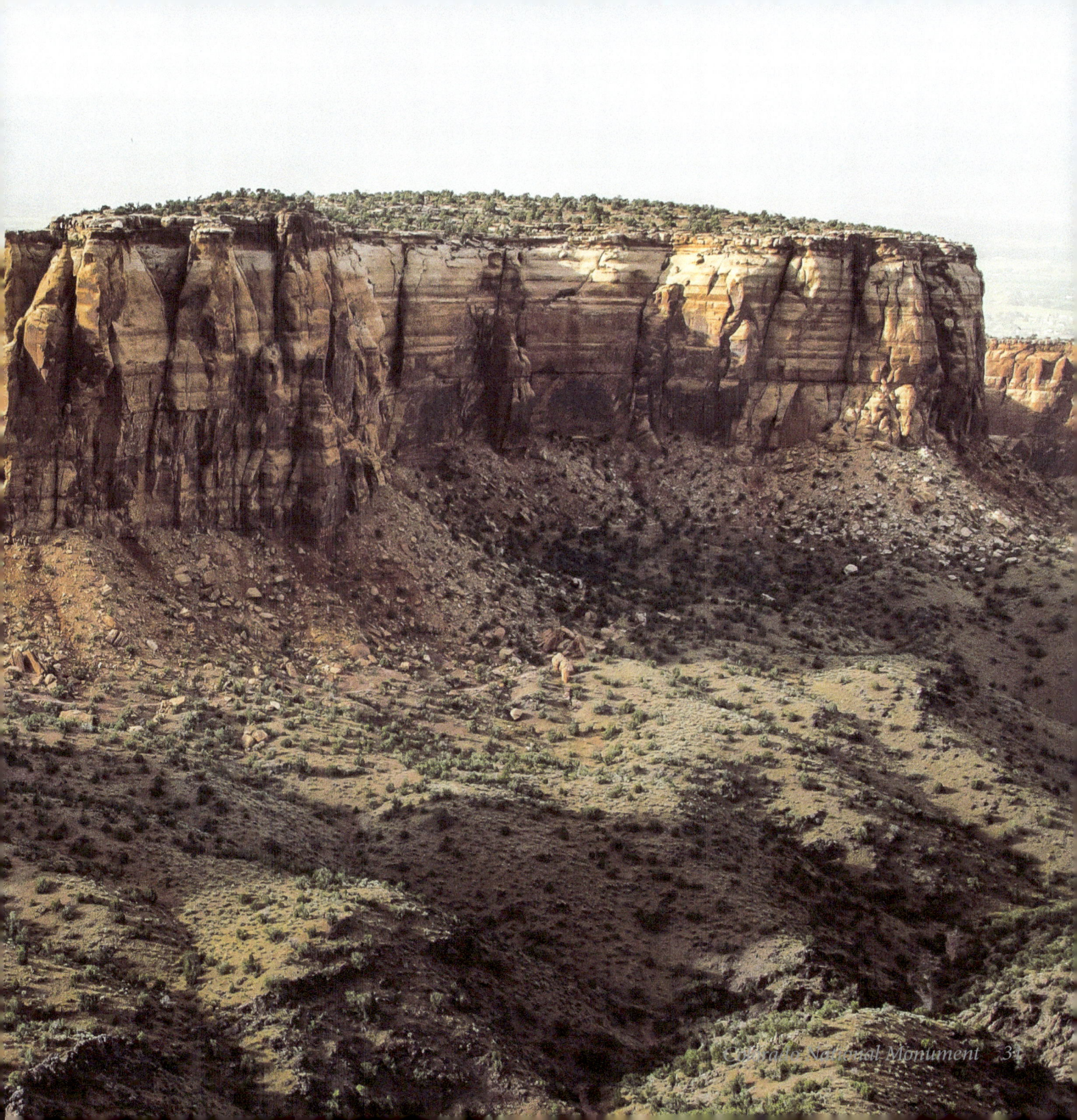

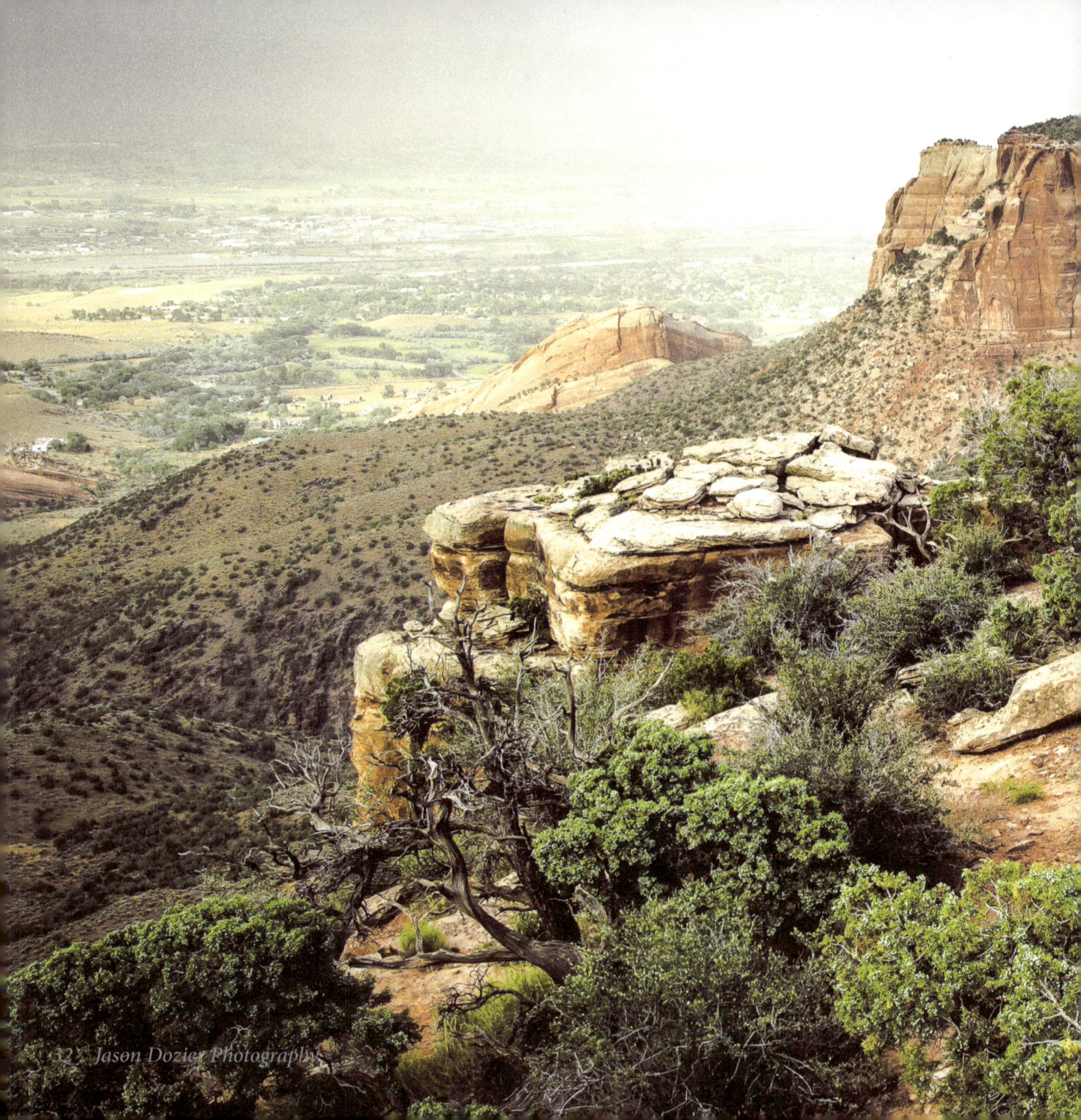

Jason Dozier Photography

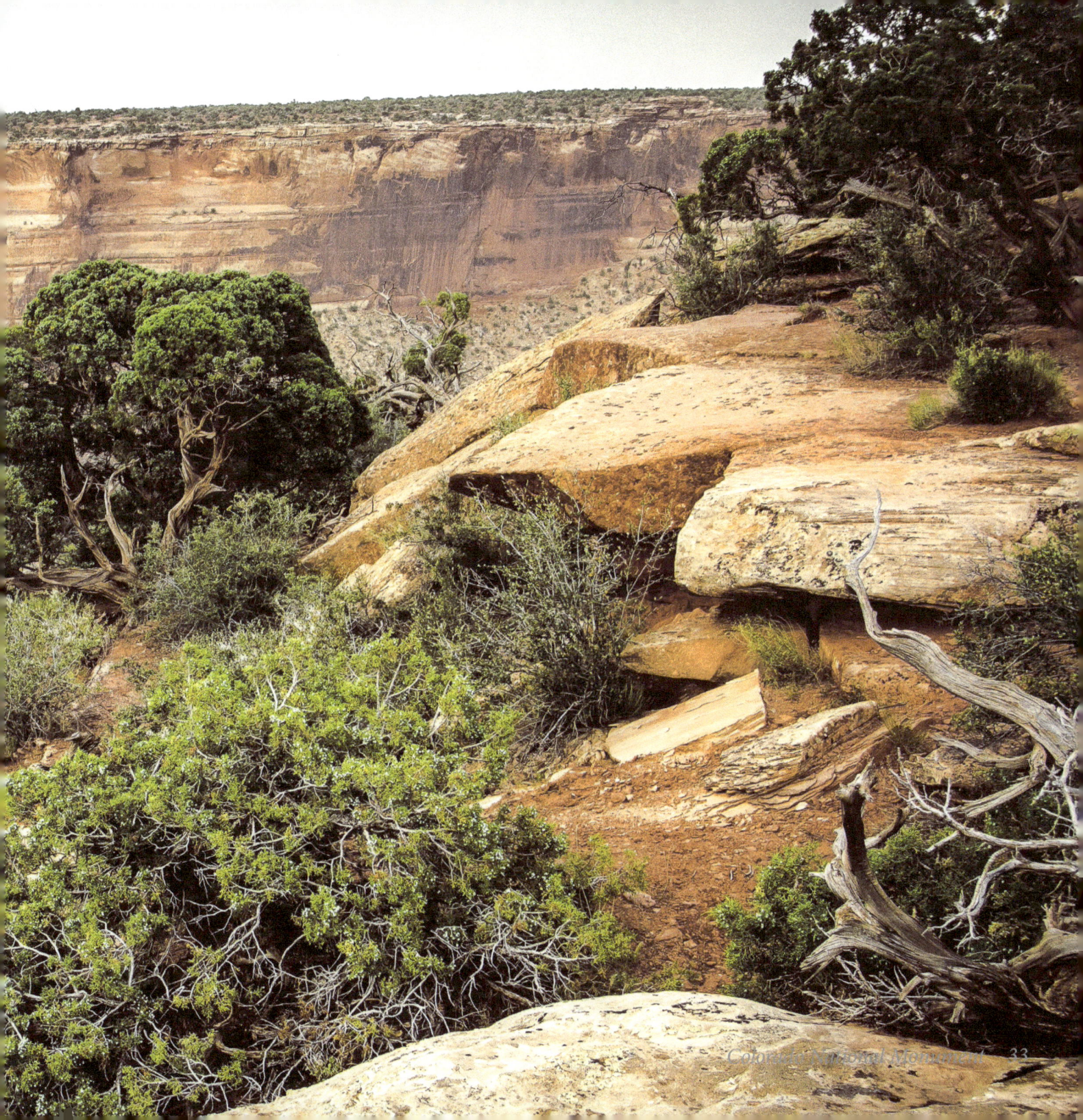

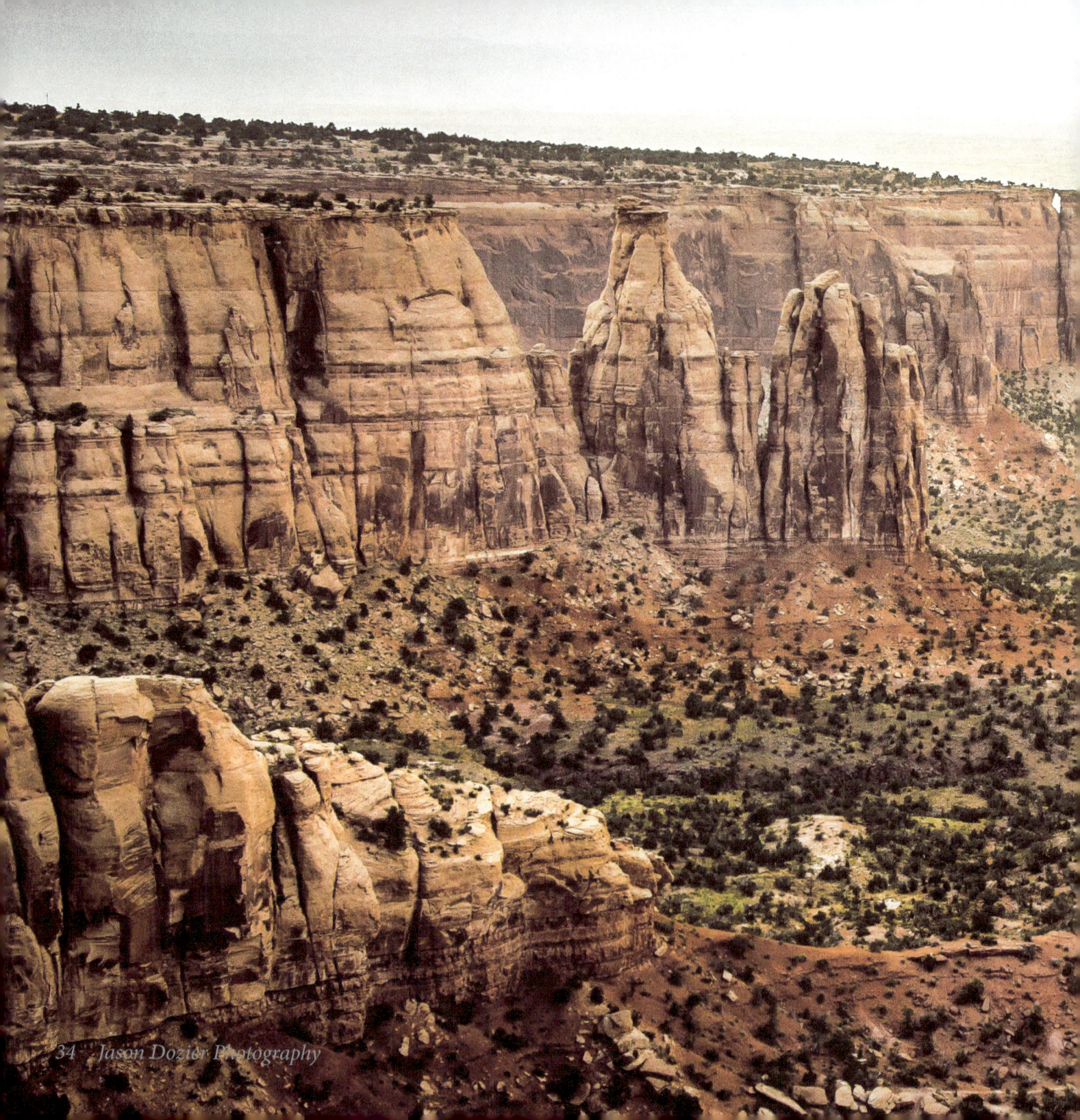

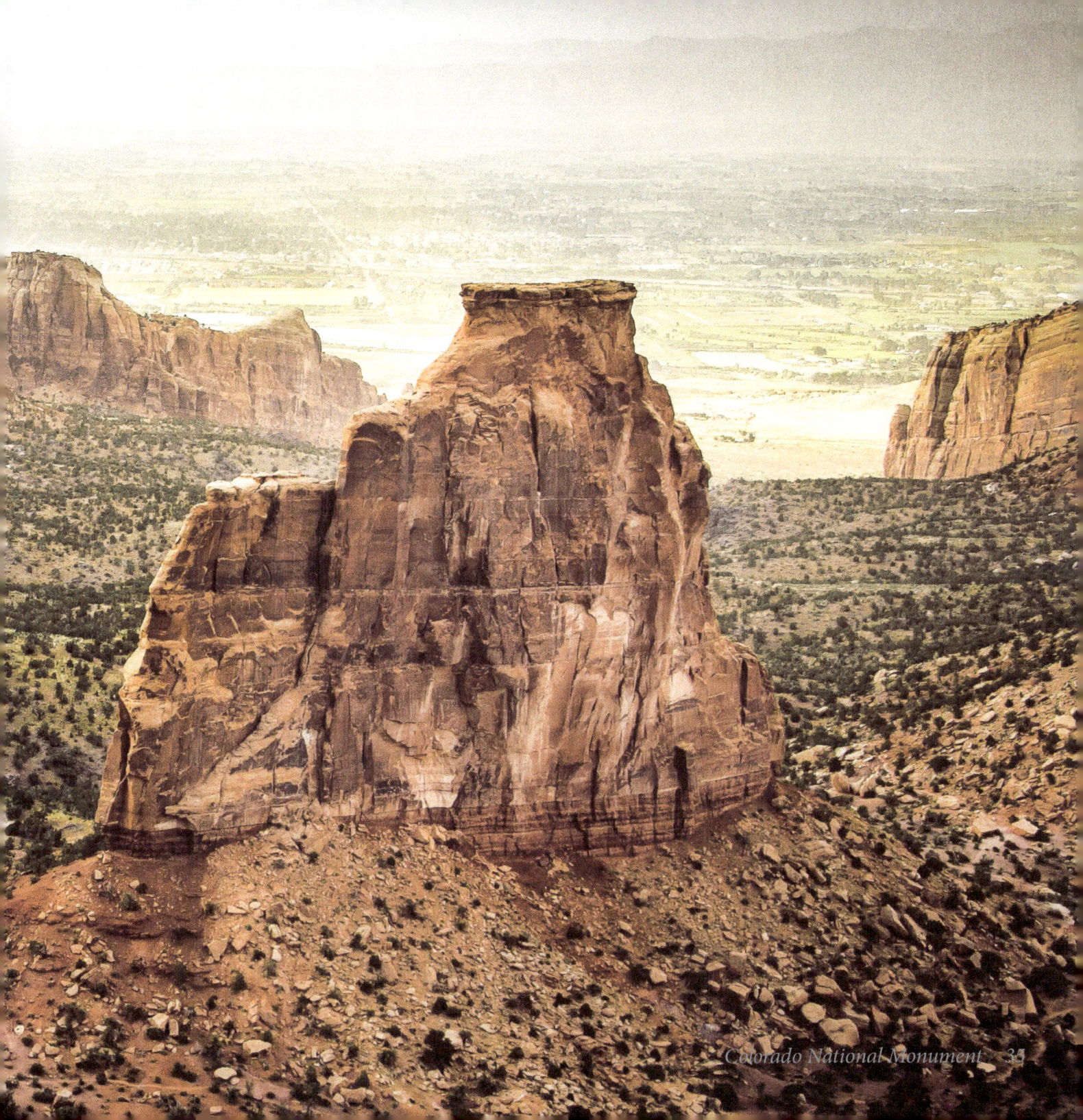

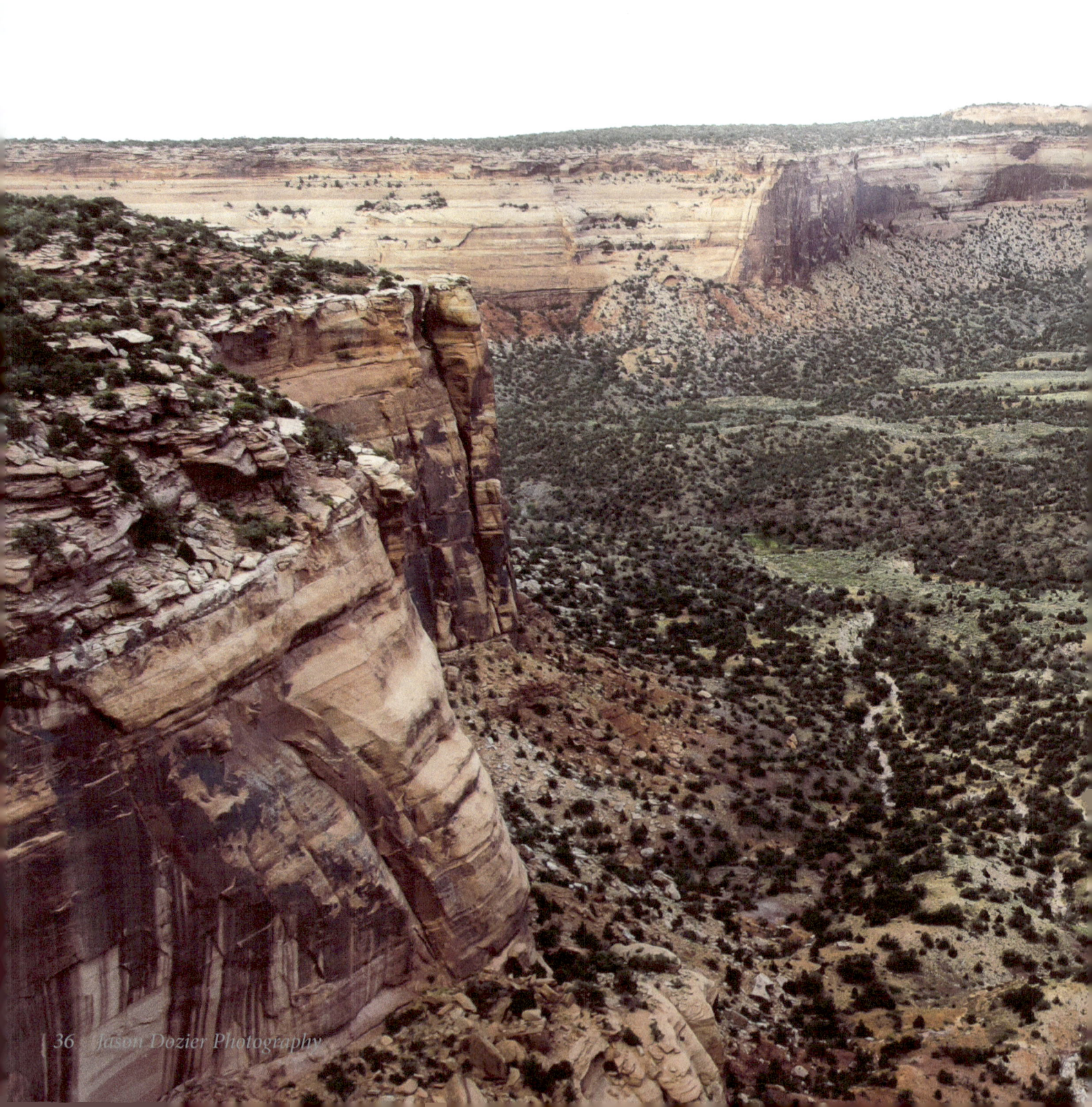

| Jason Dozier Photography

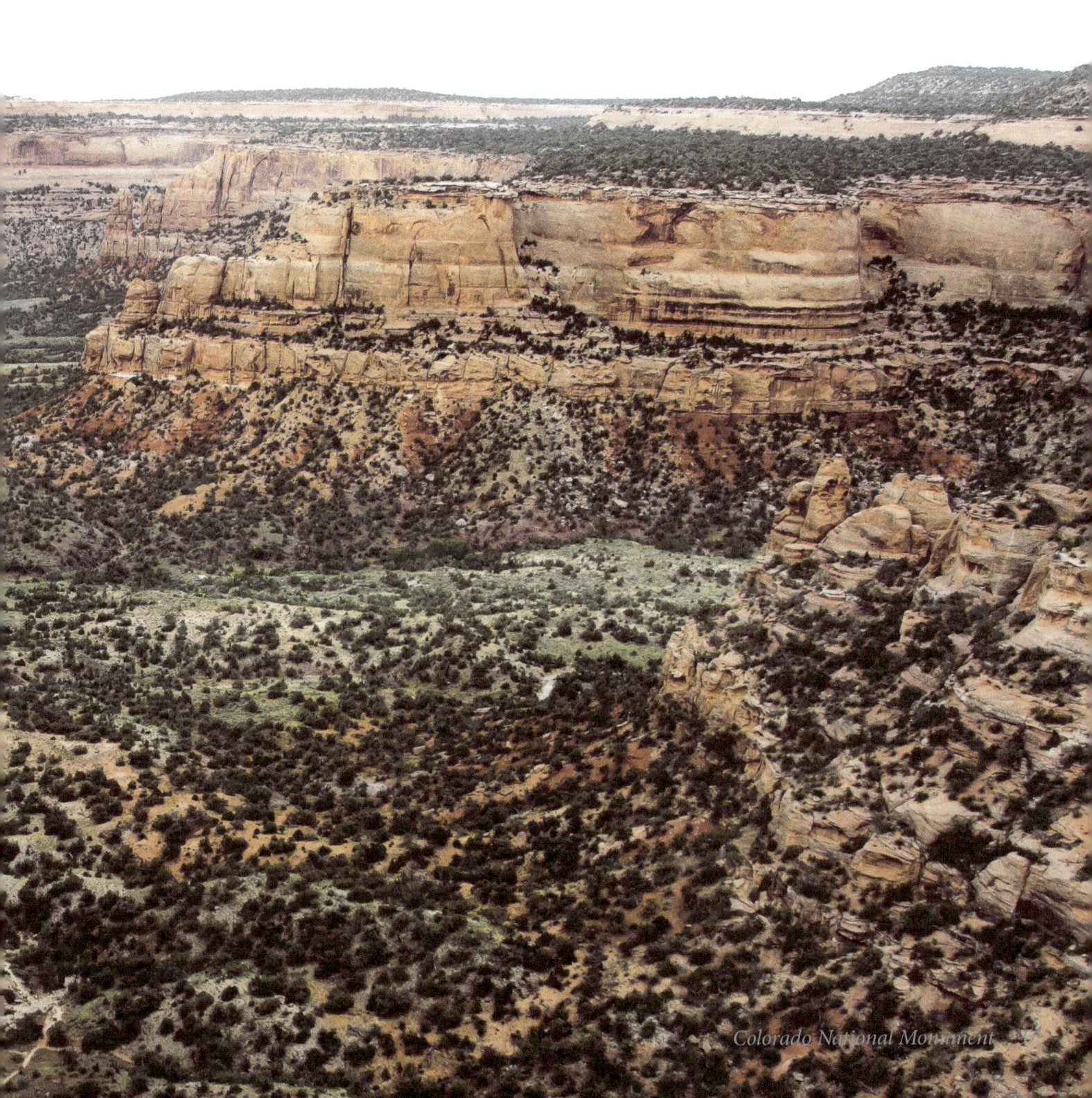

Colorado National Monument

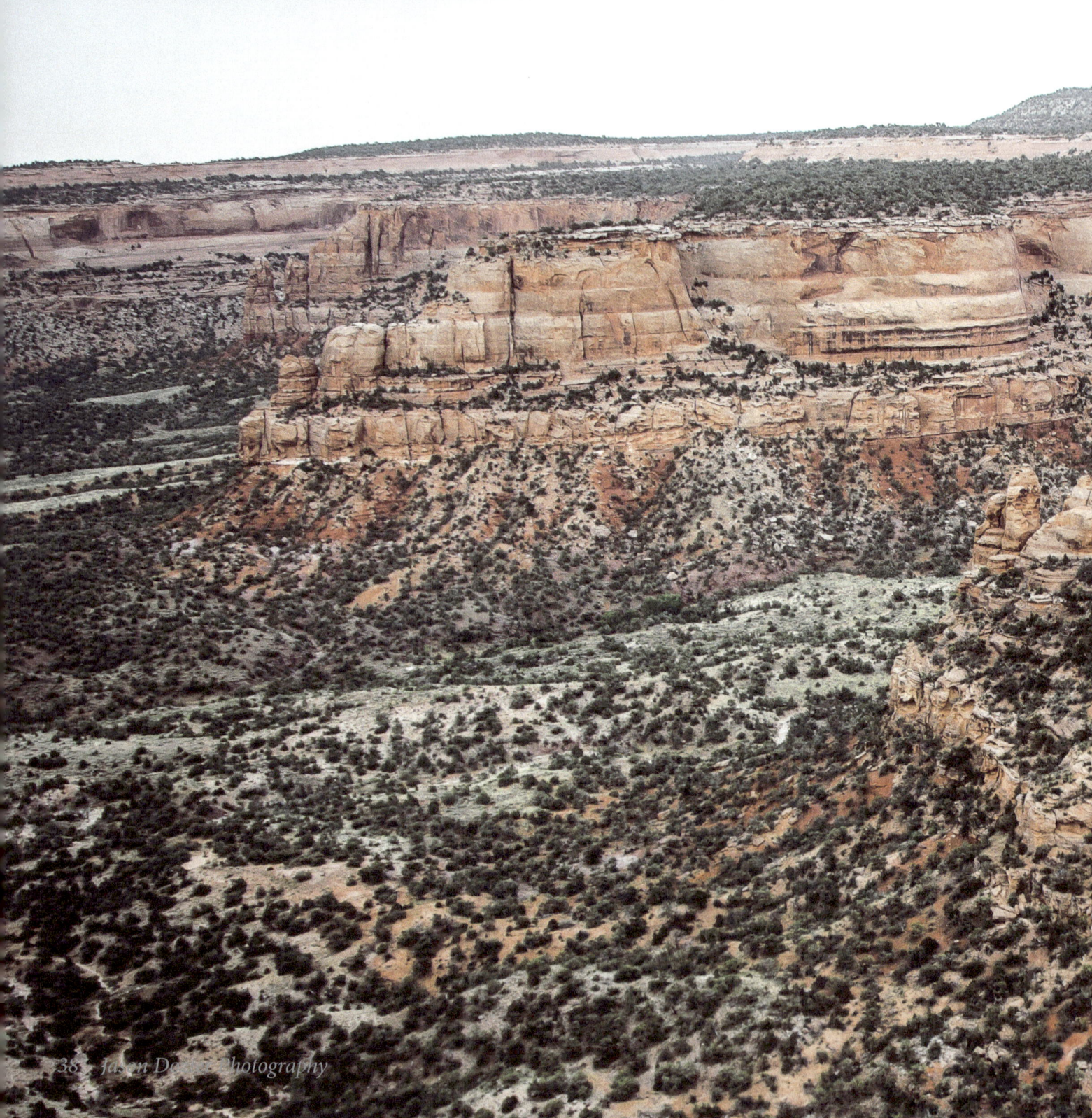

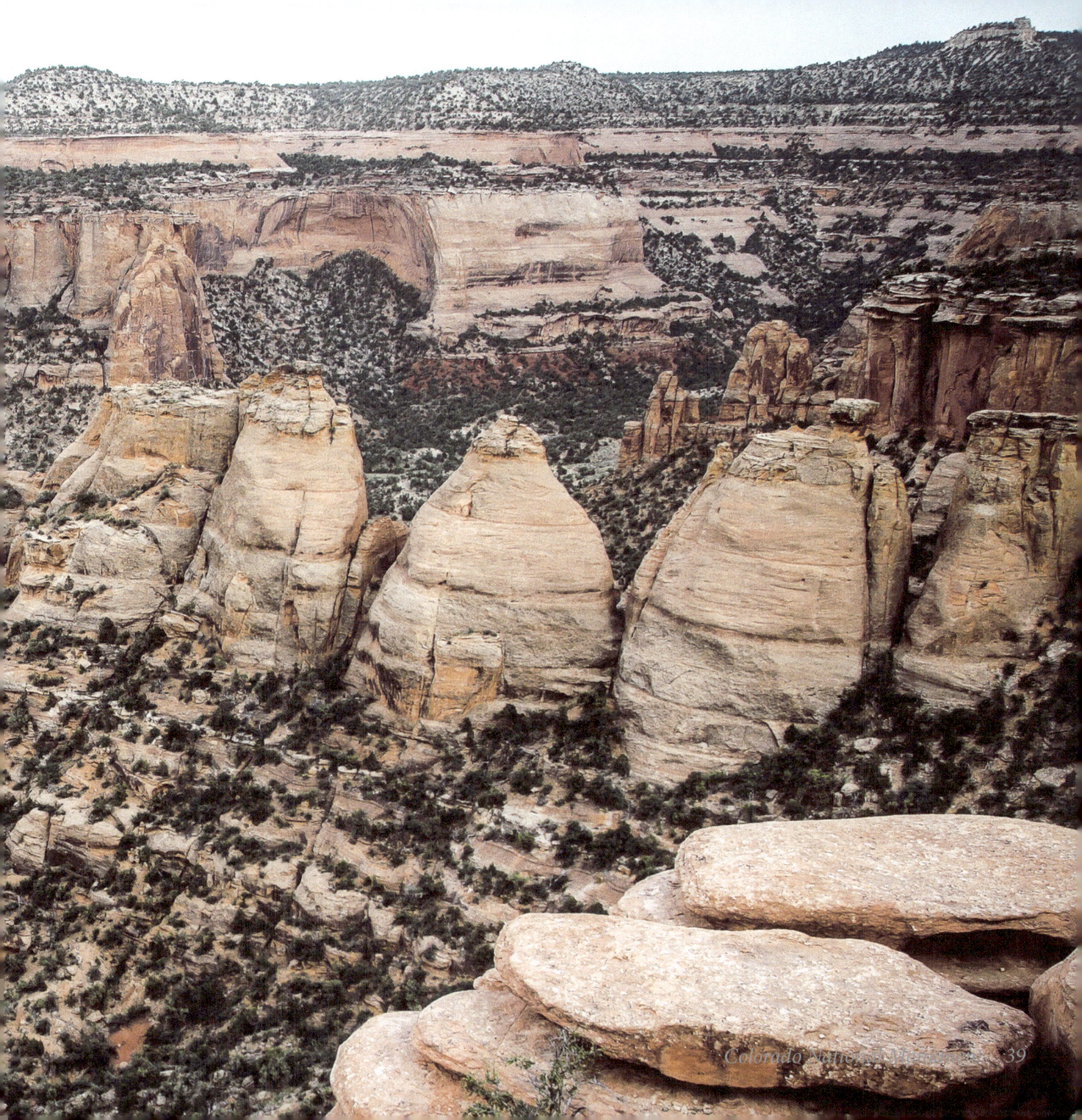

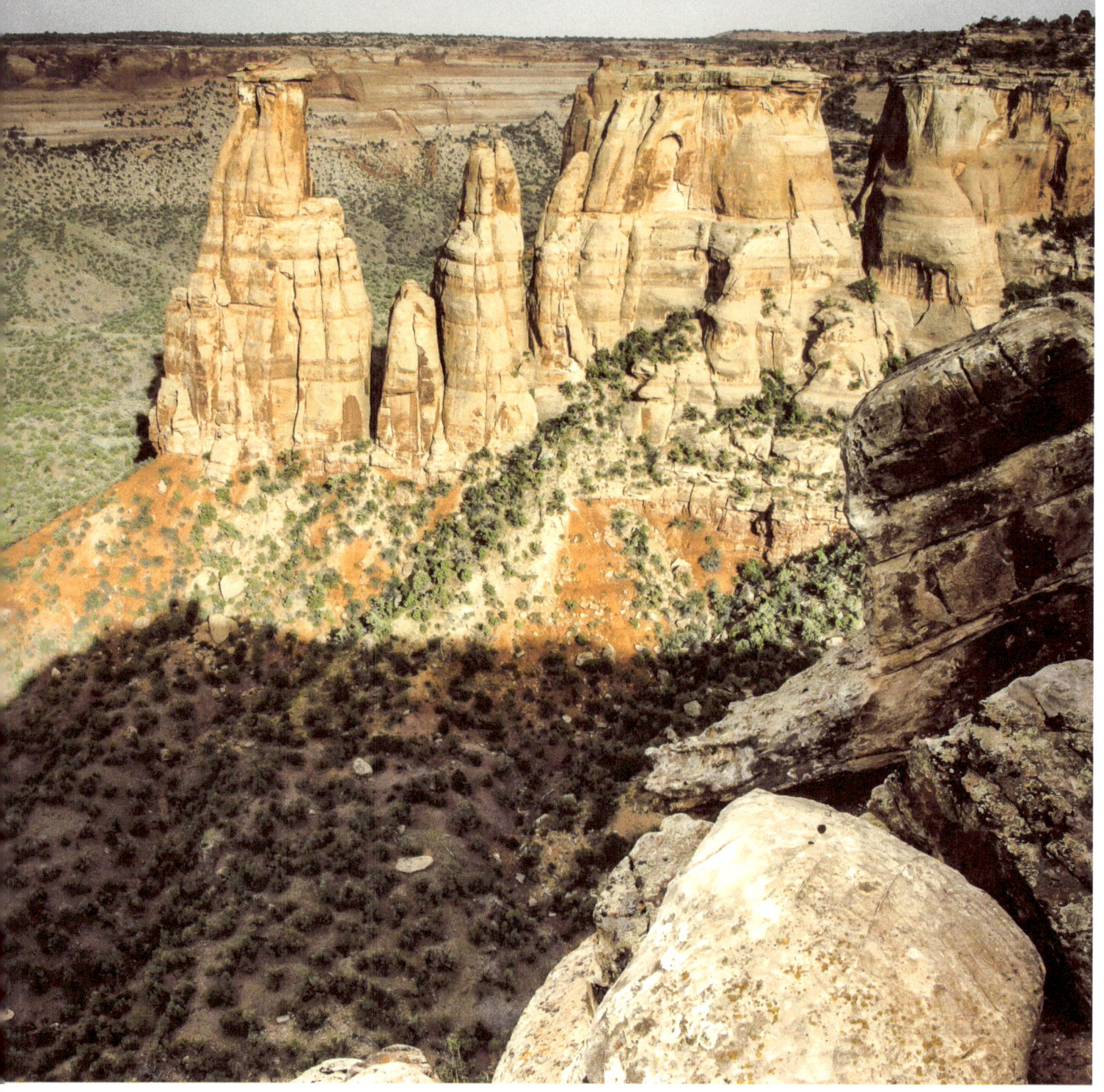

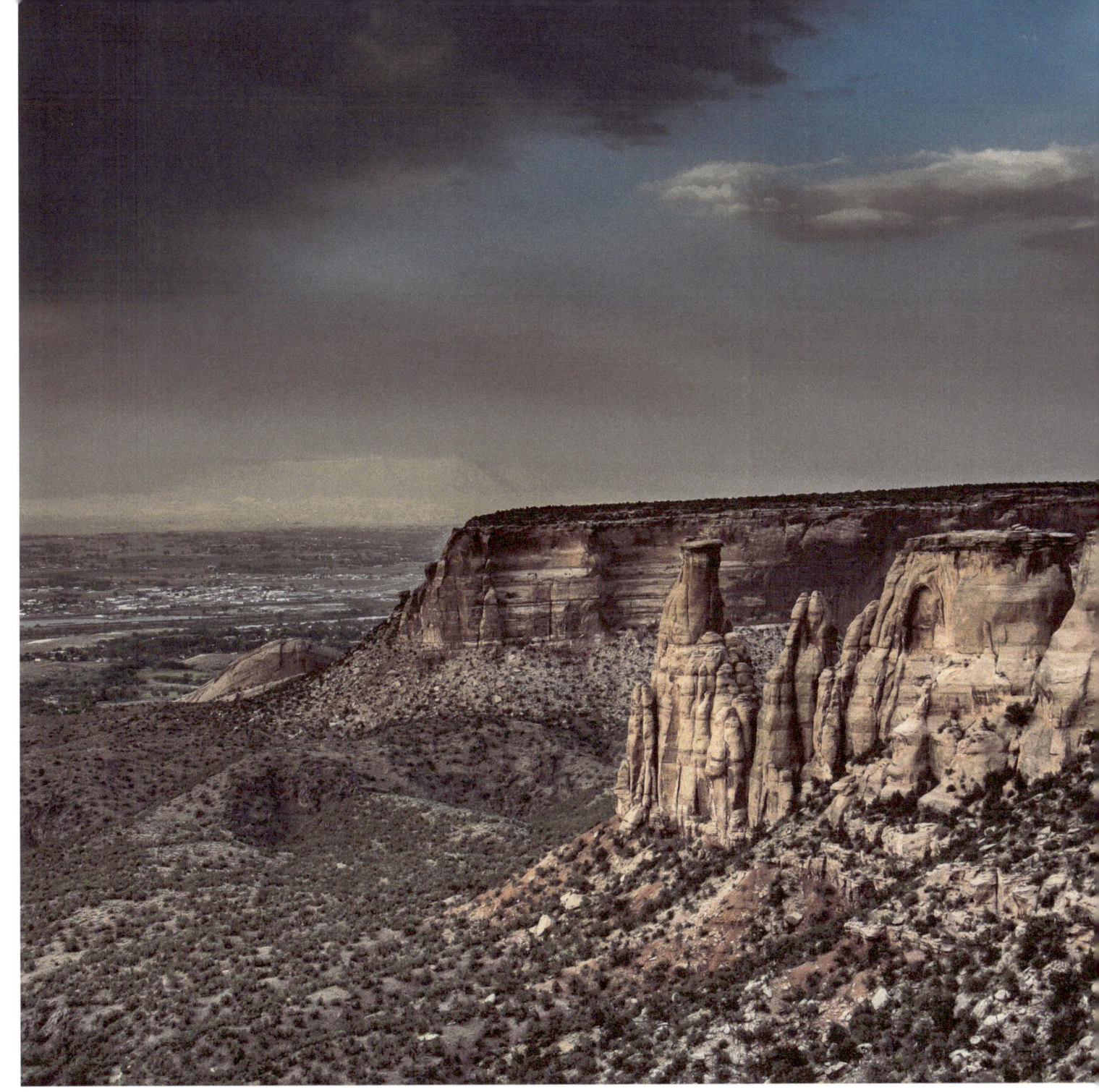

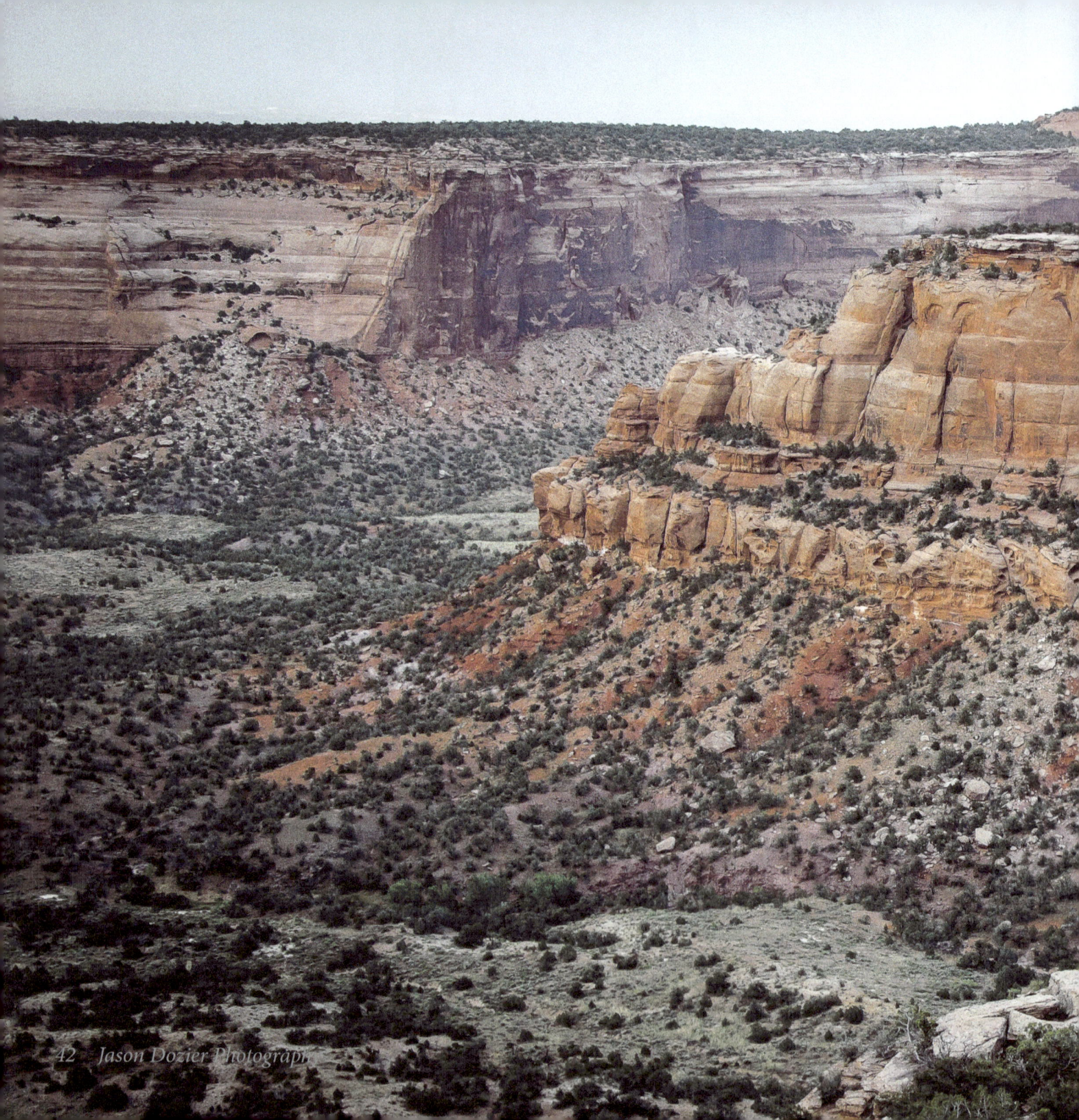

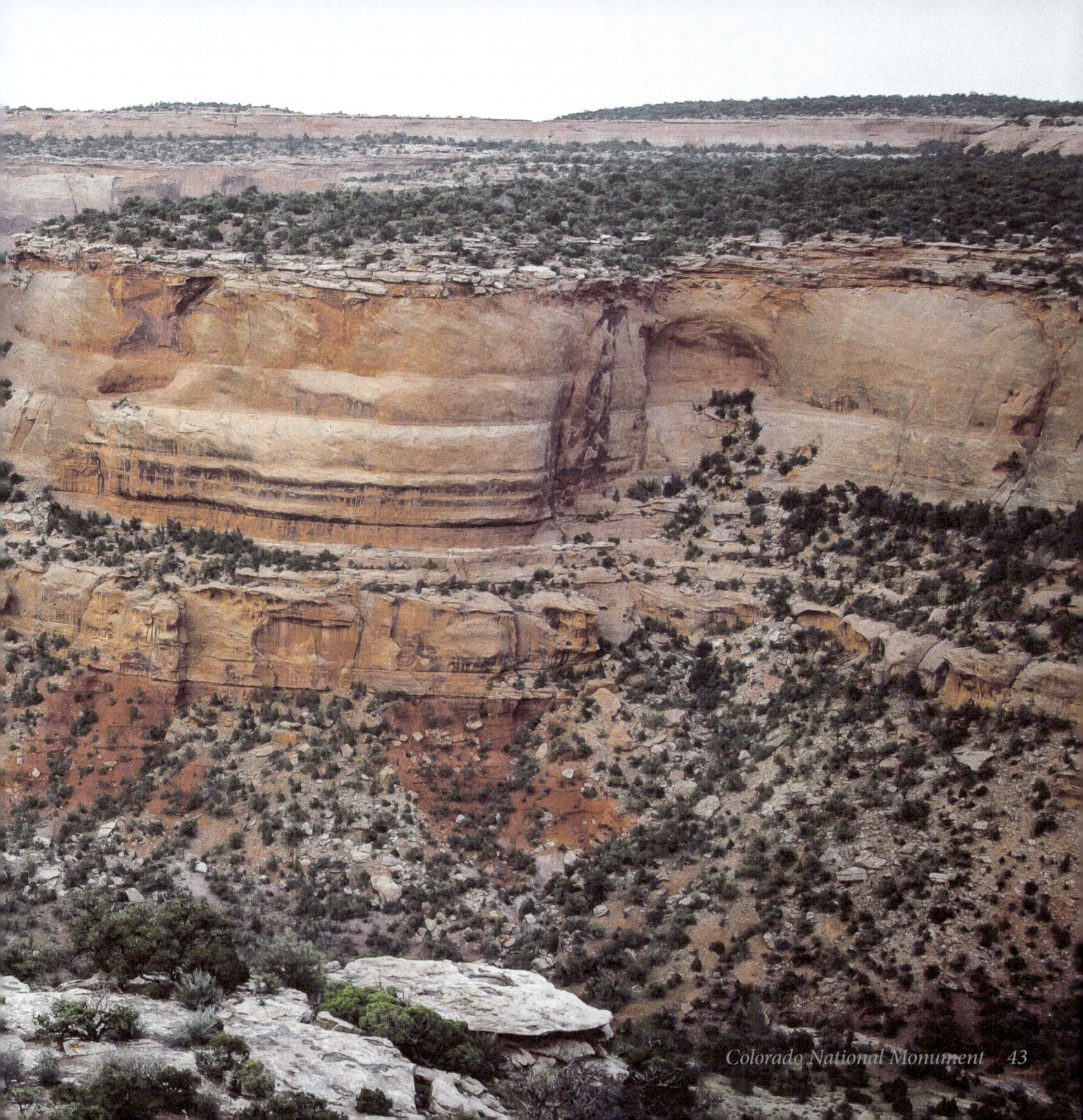

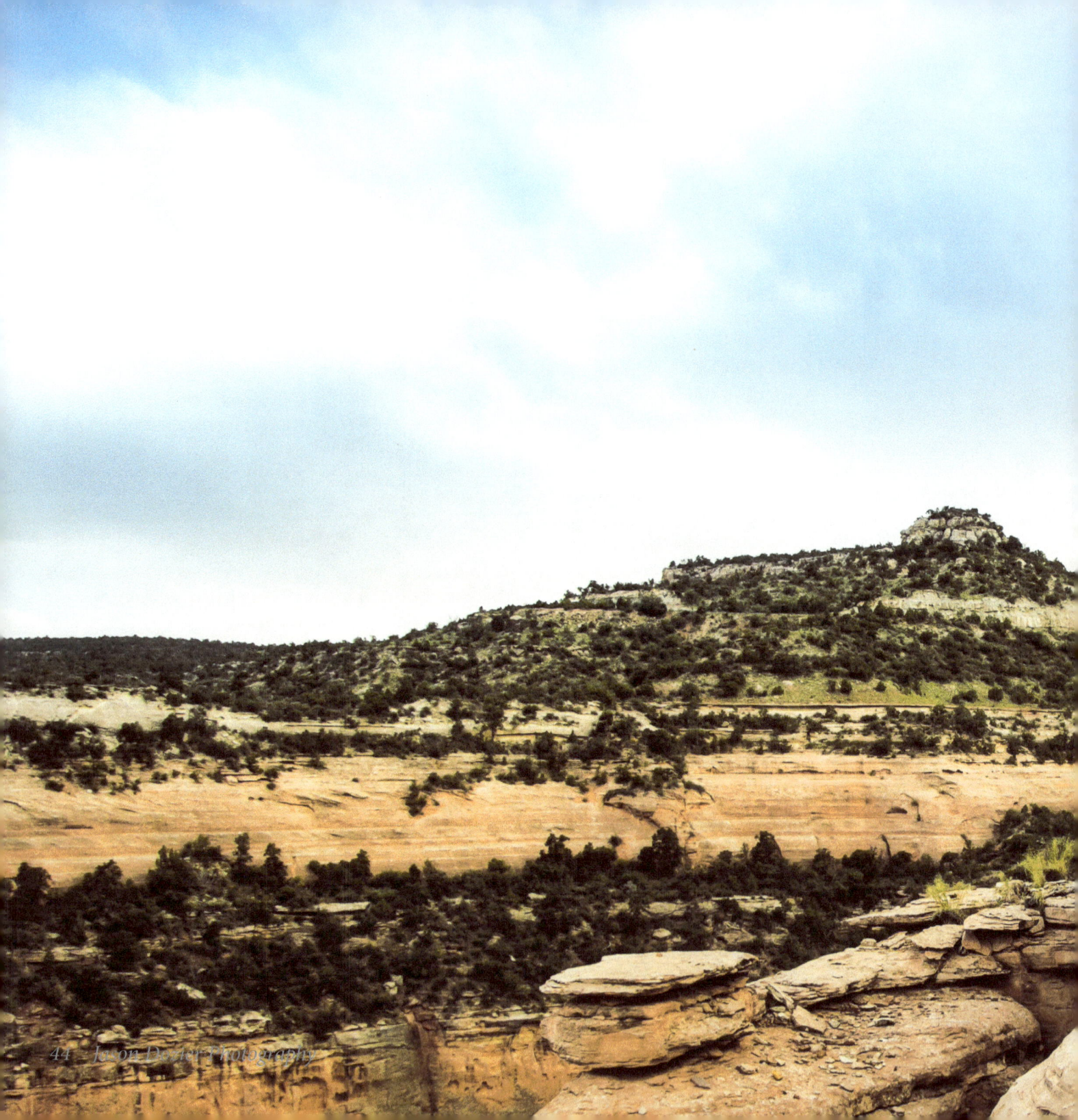

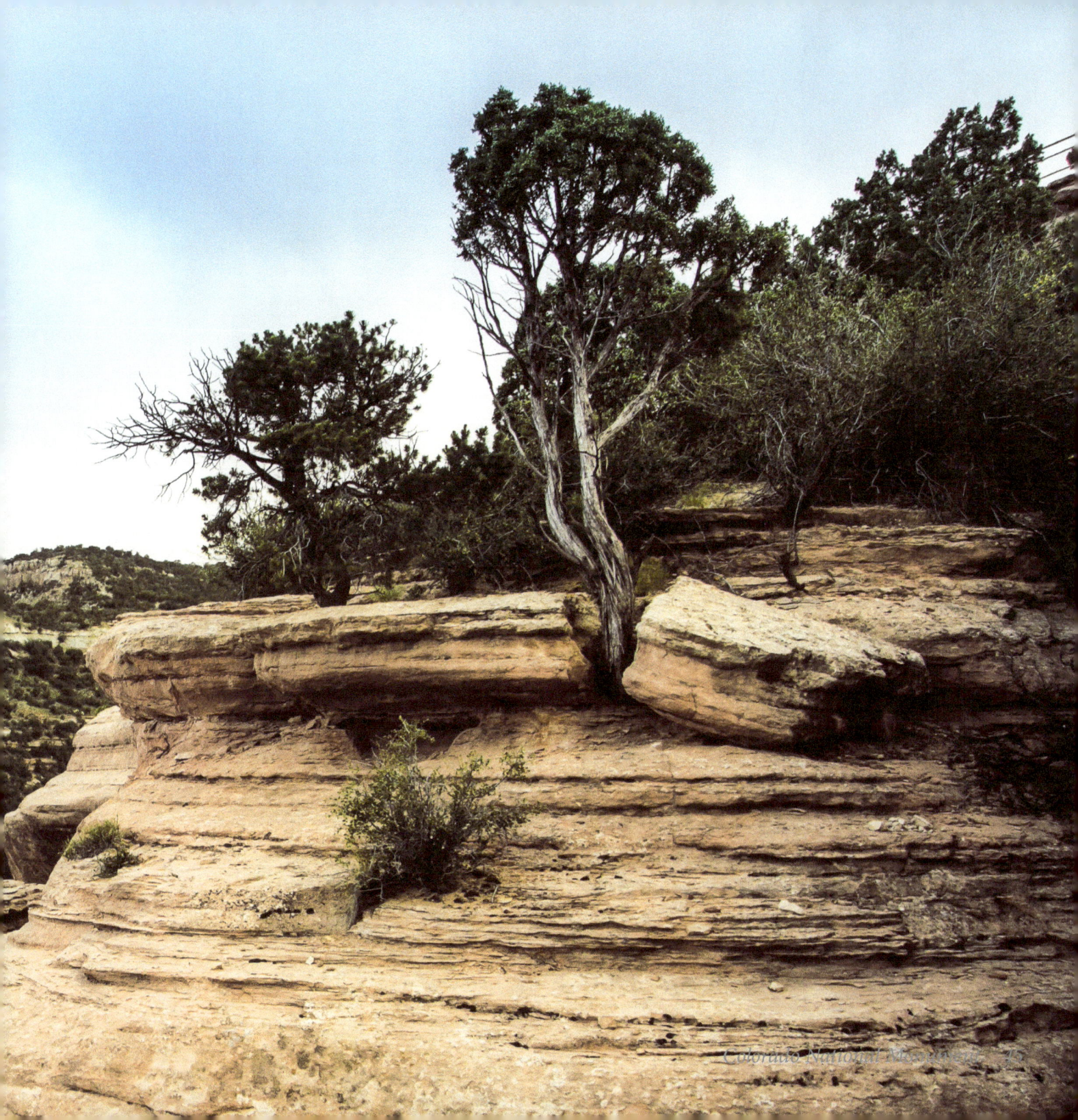

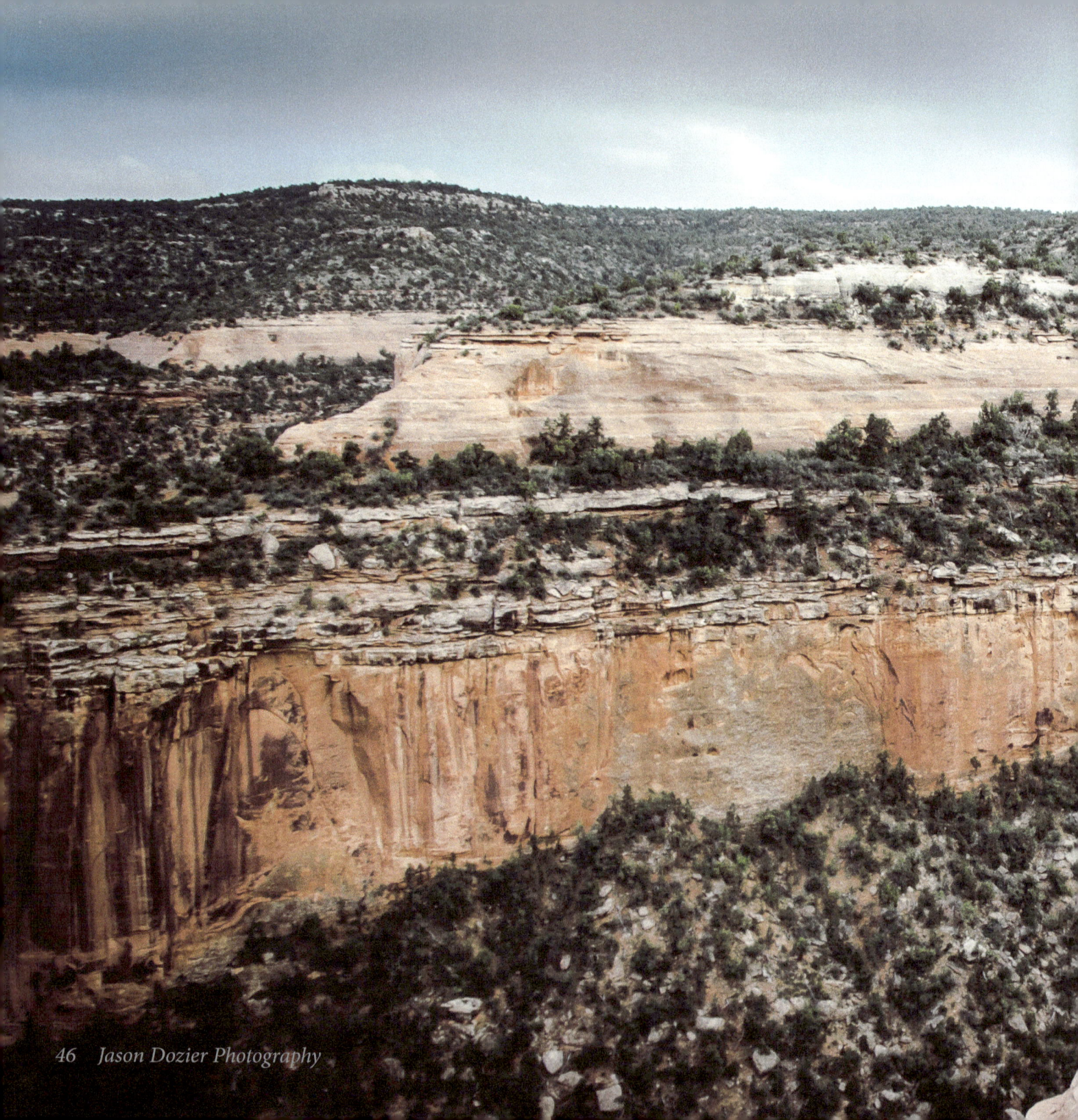

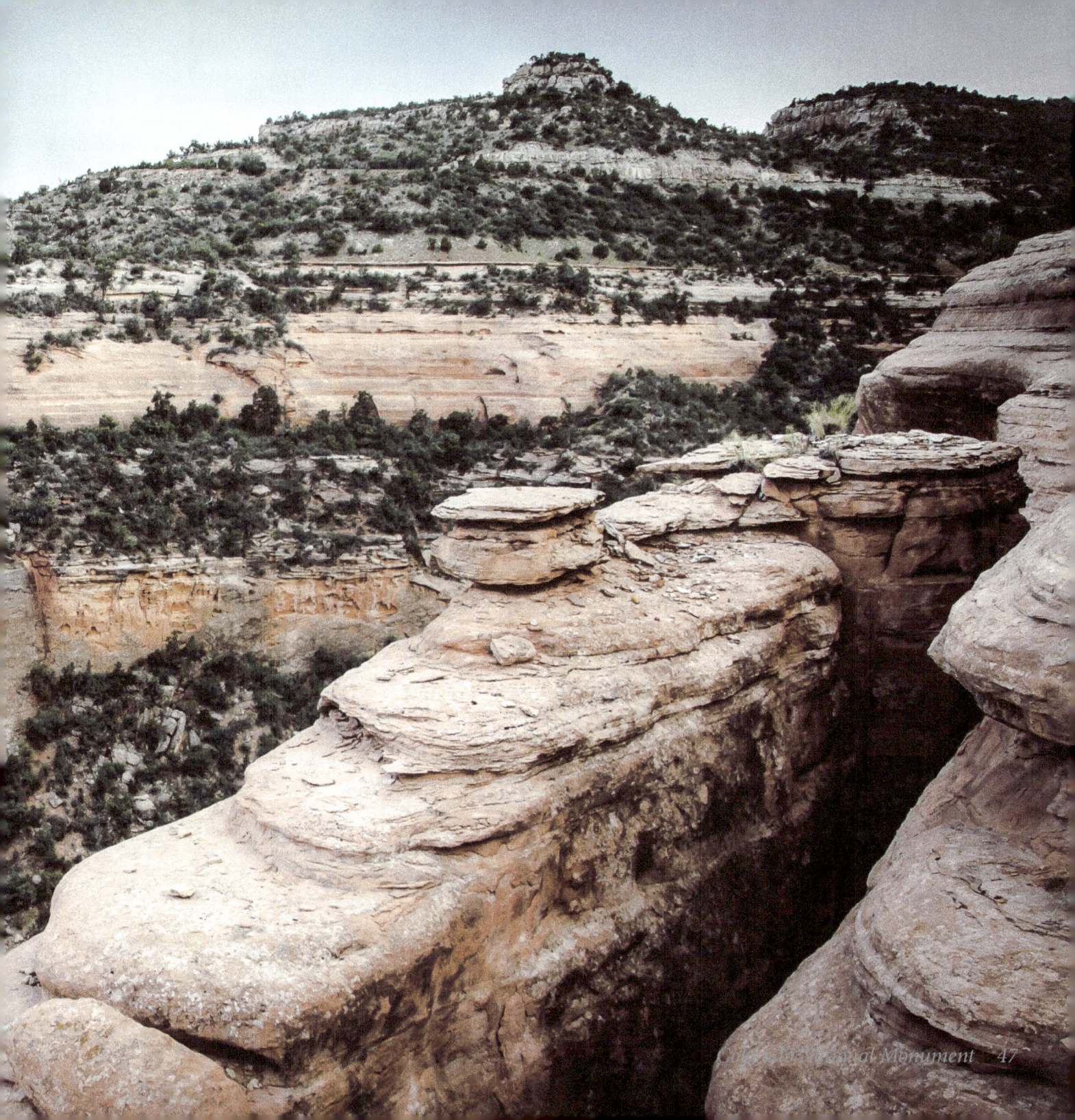

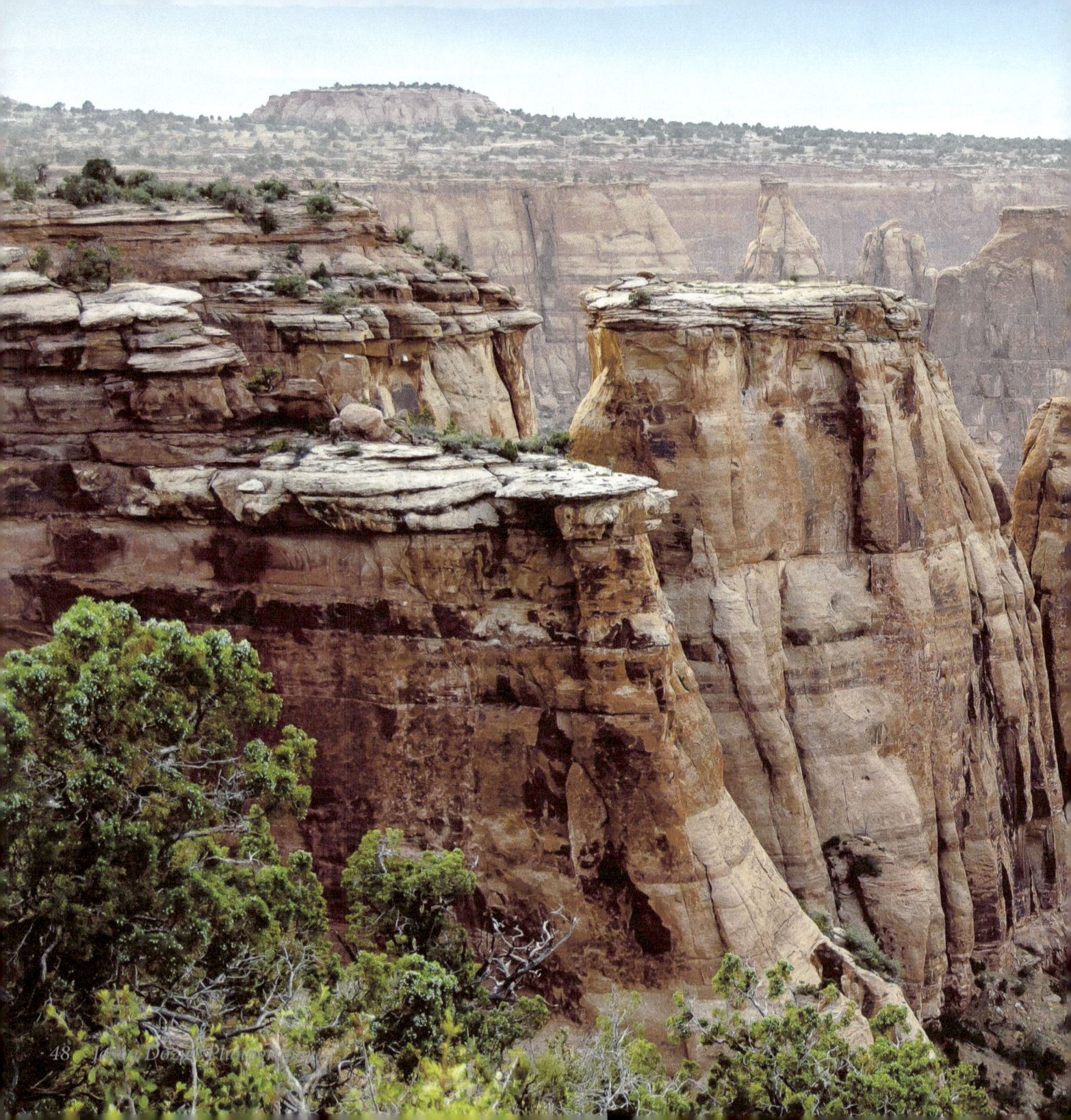

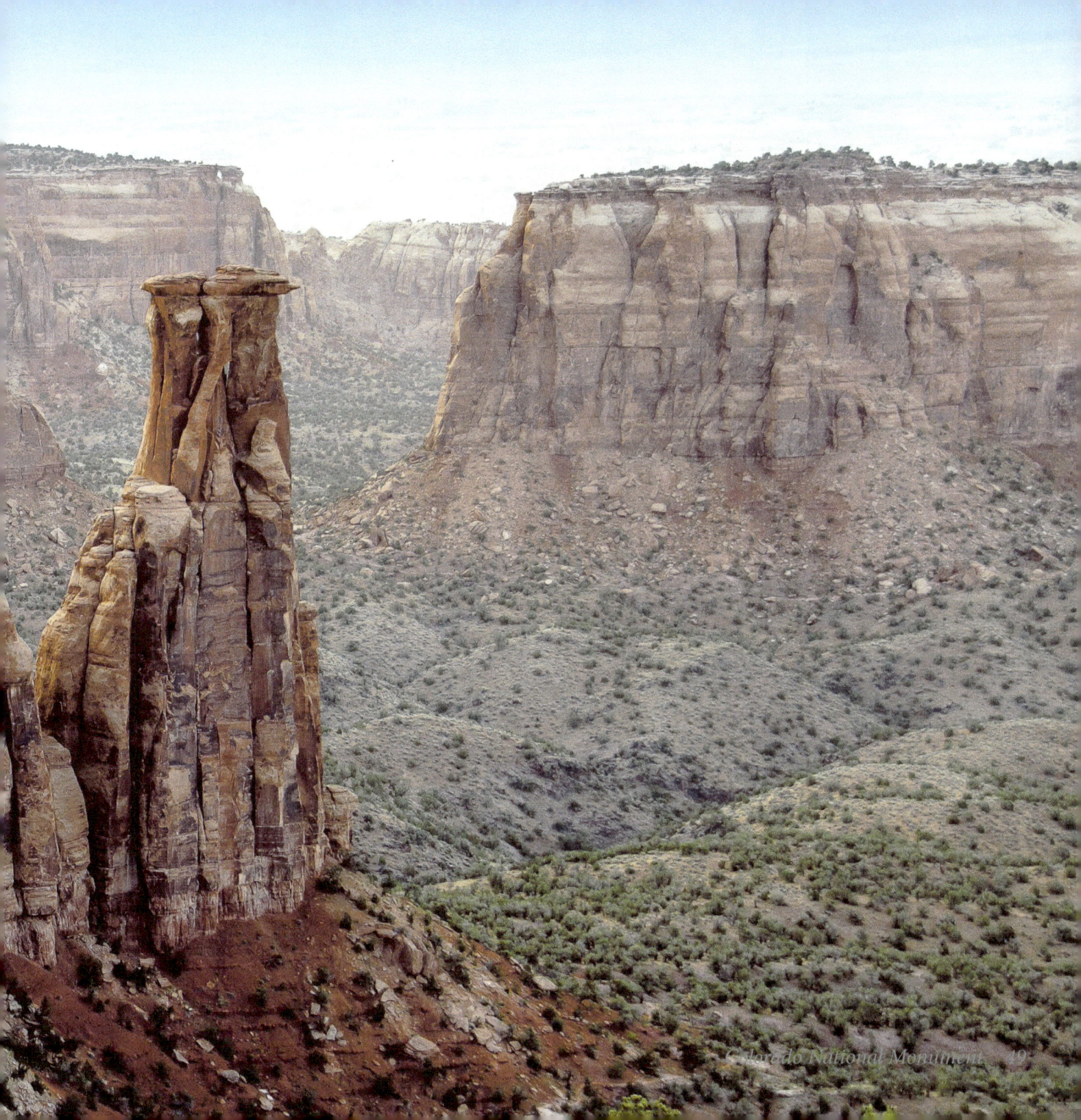

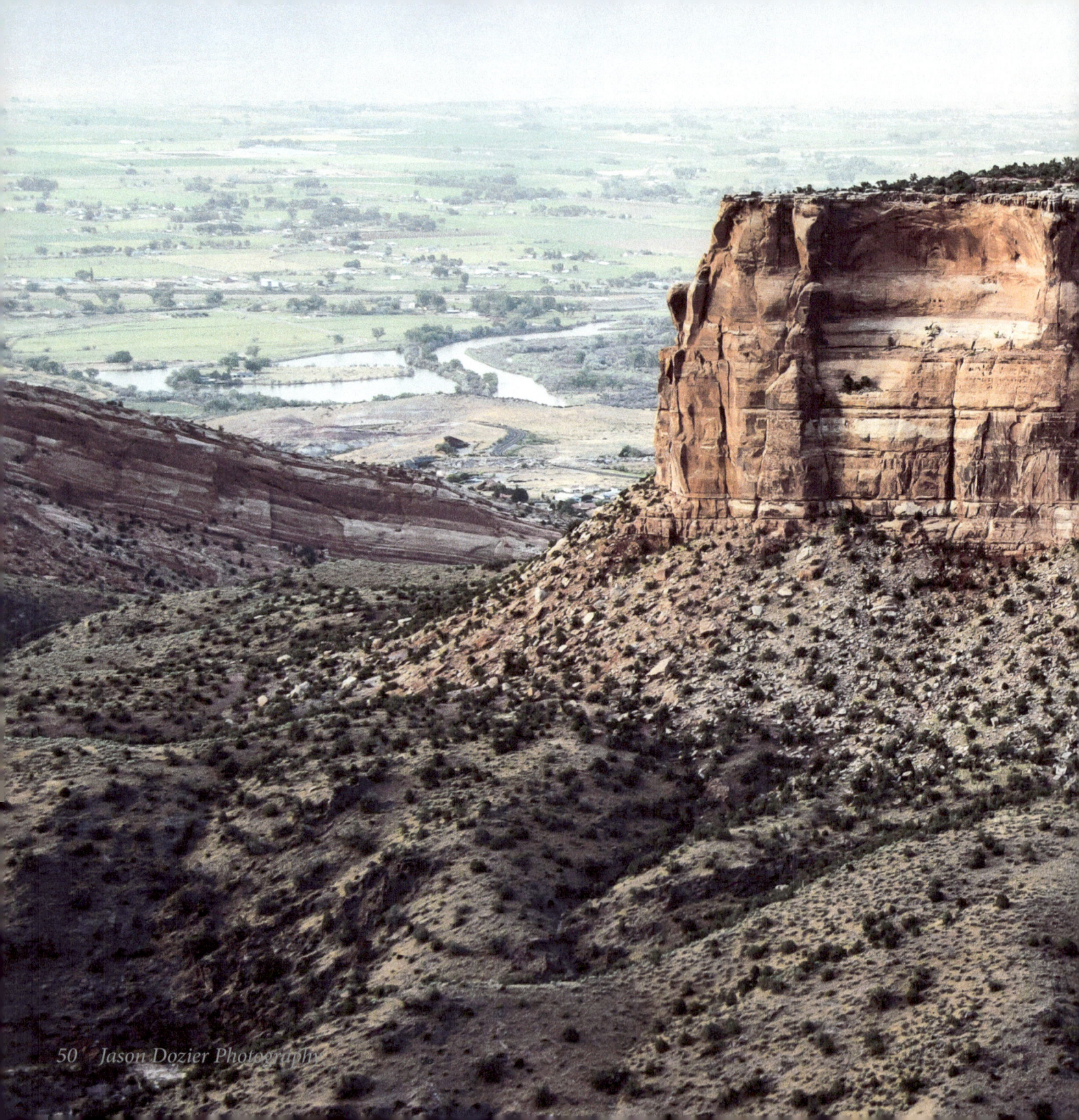

Jason Dozier Photography

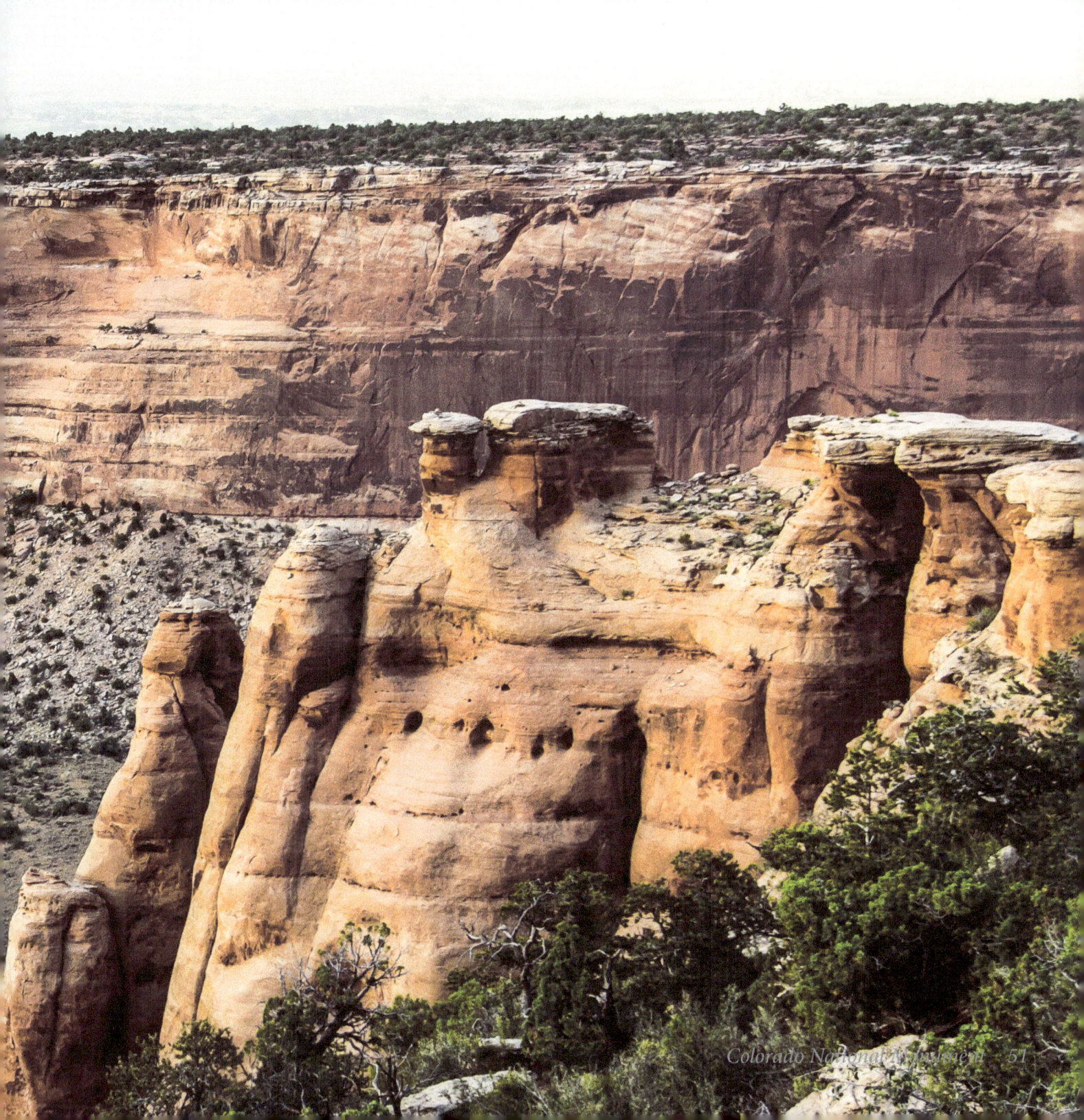

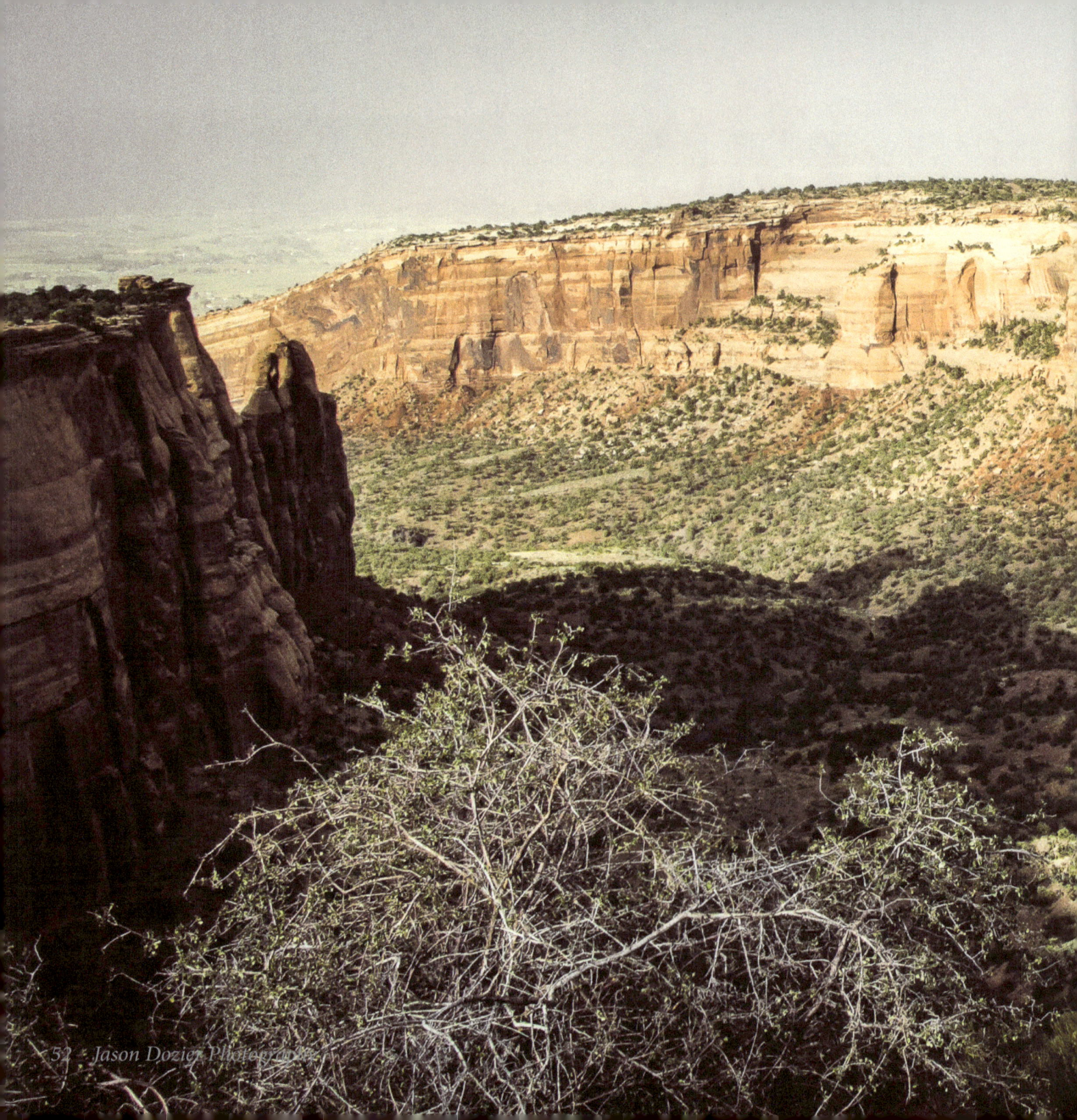

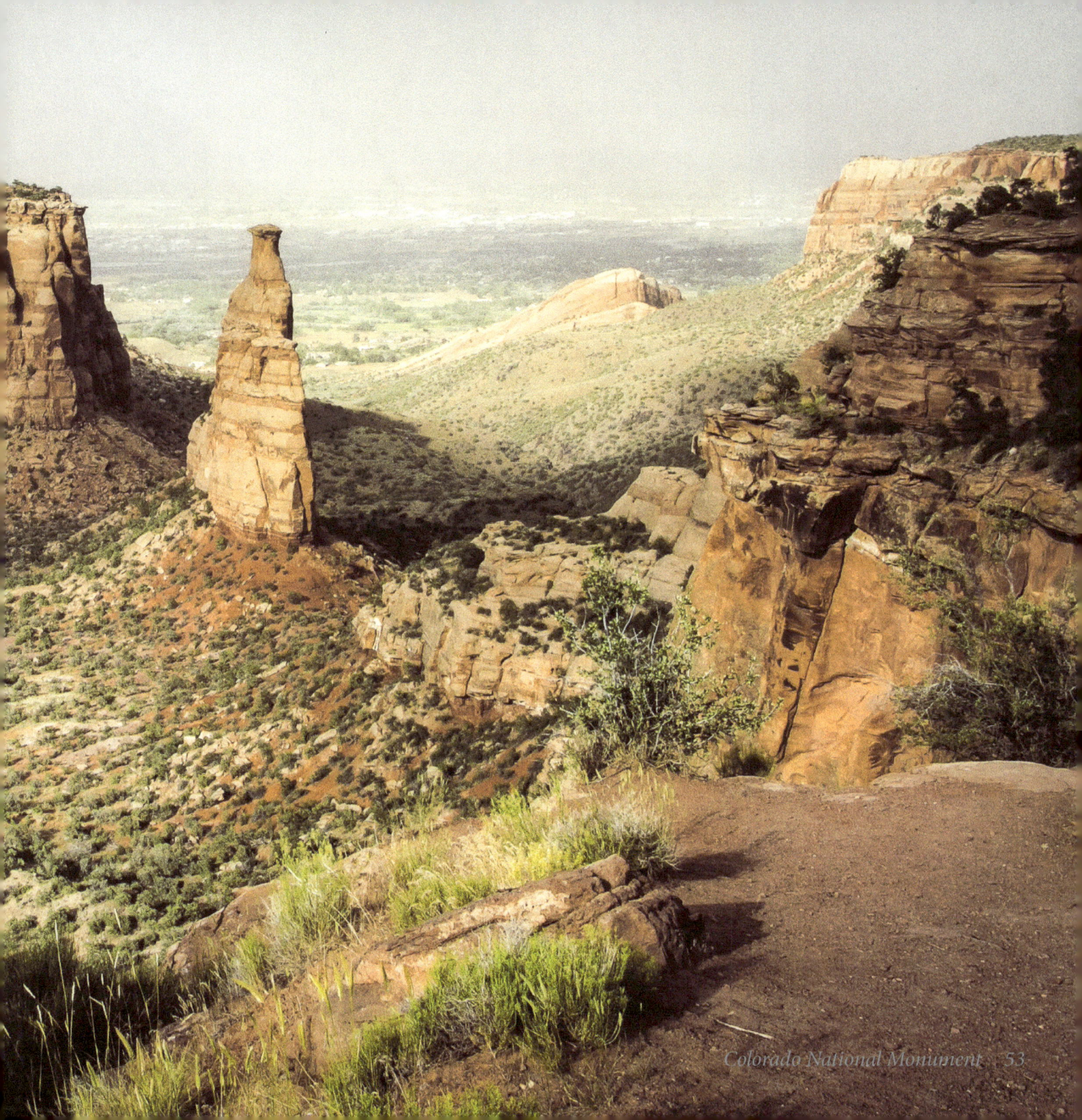

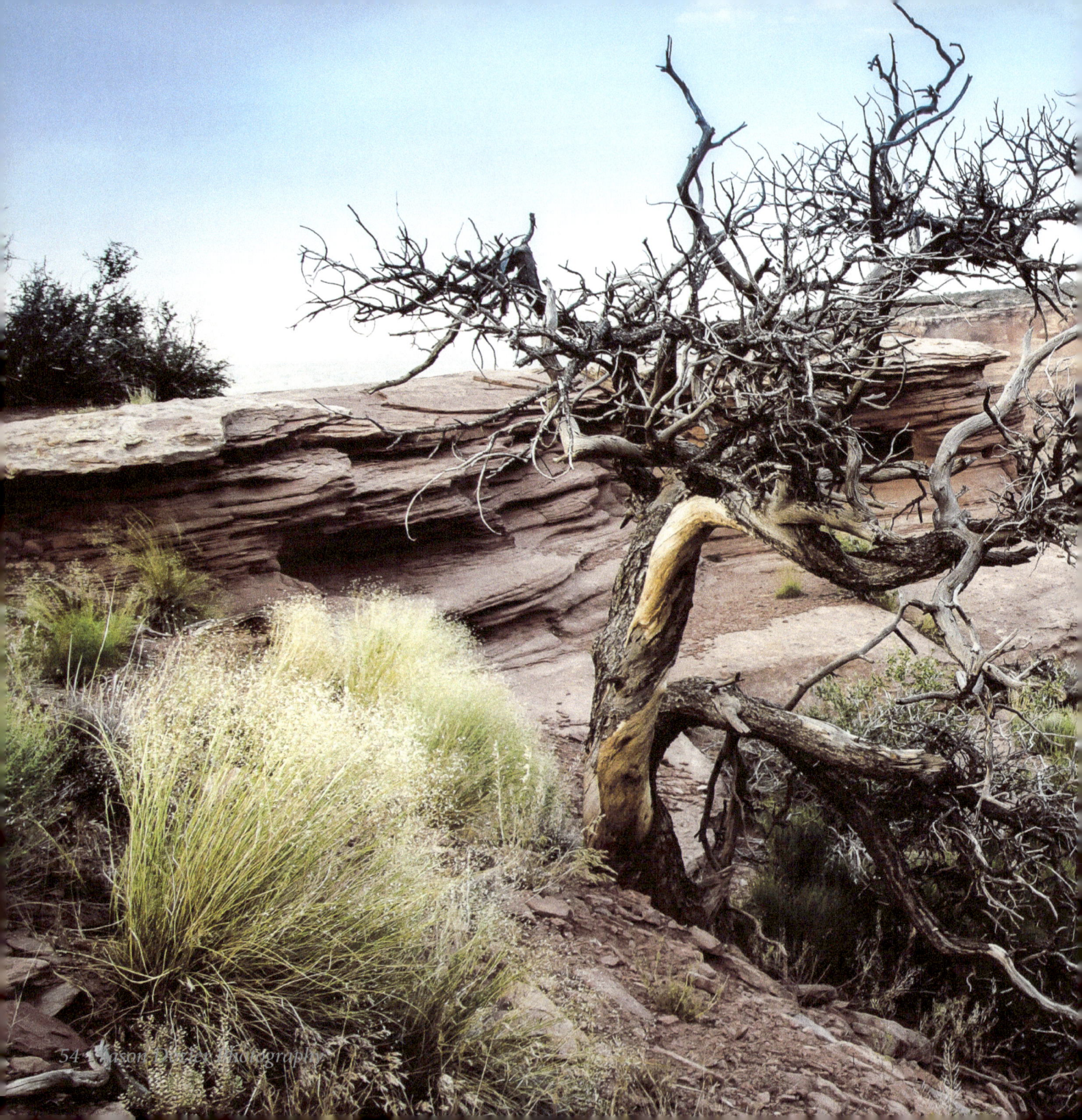

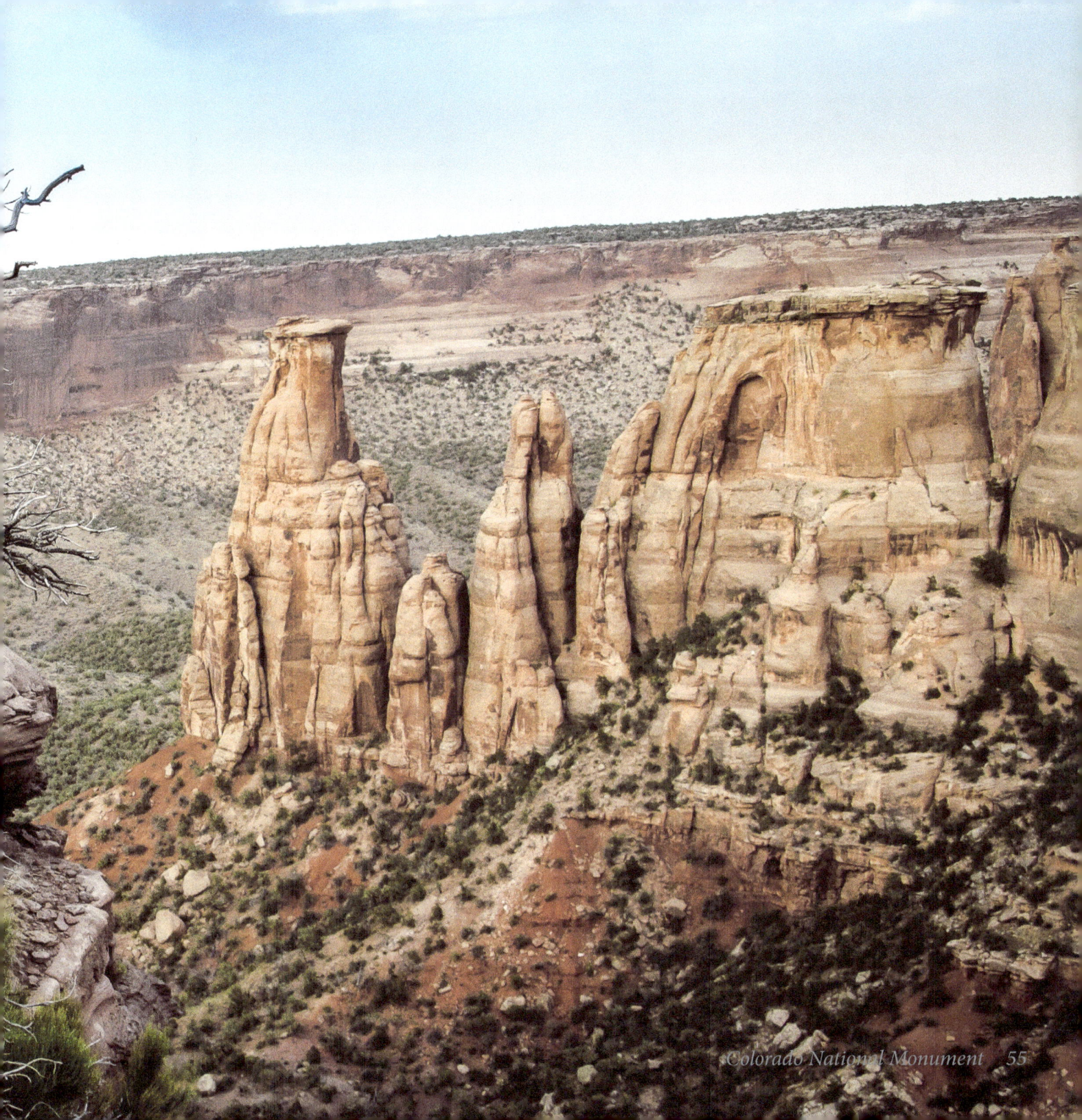

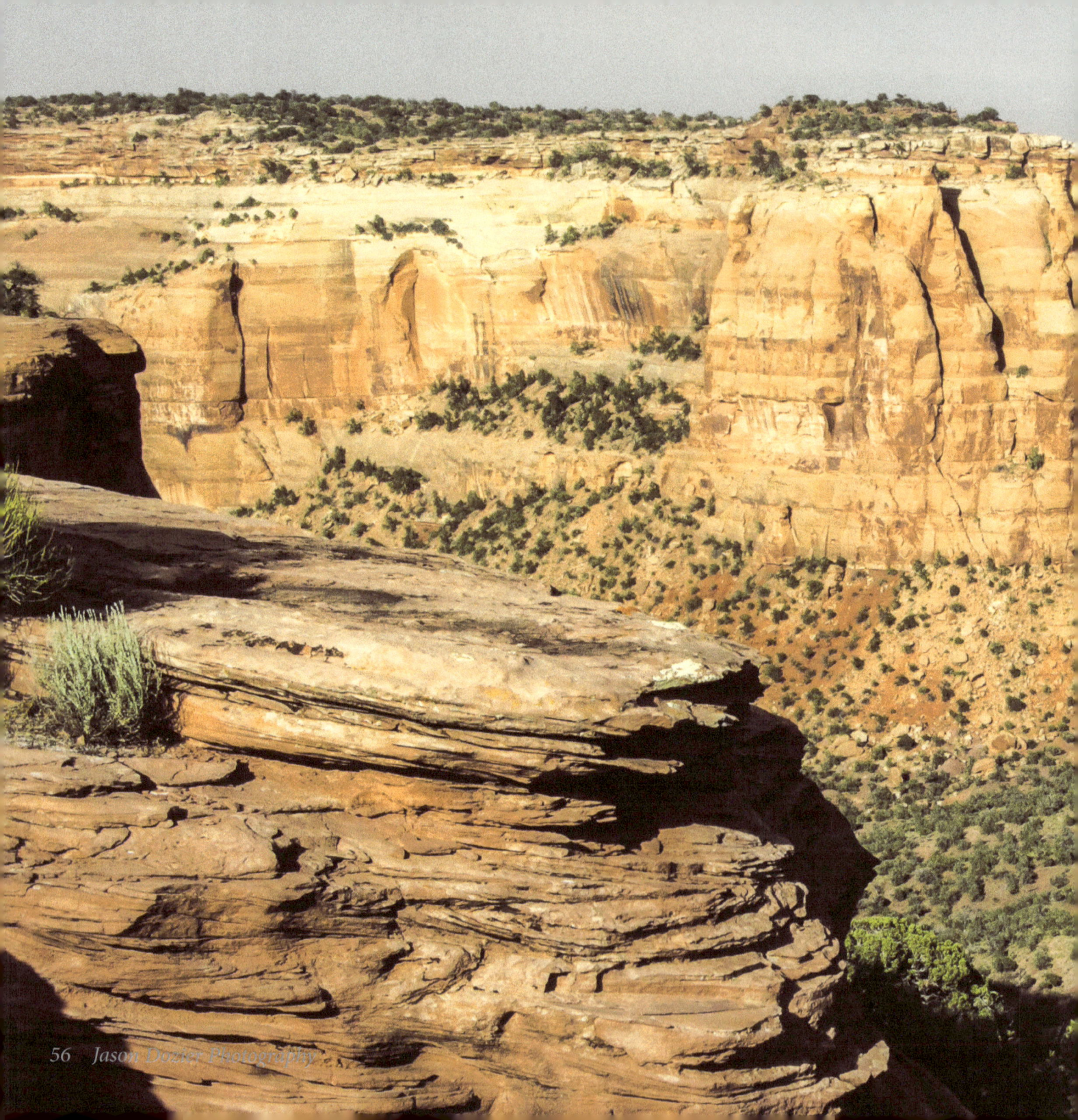

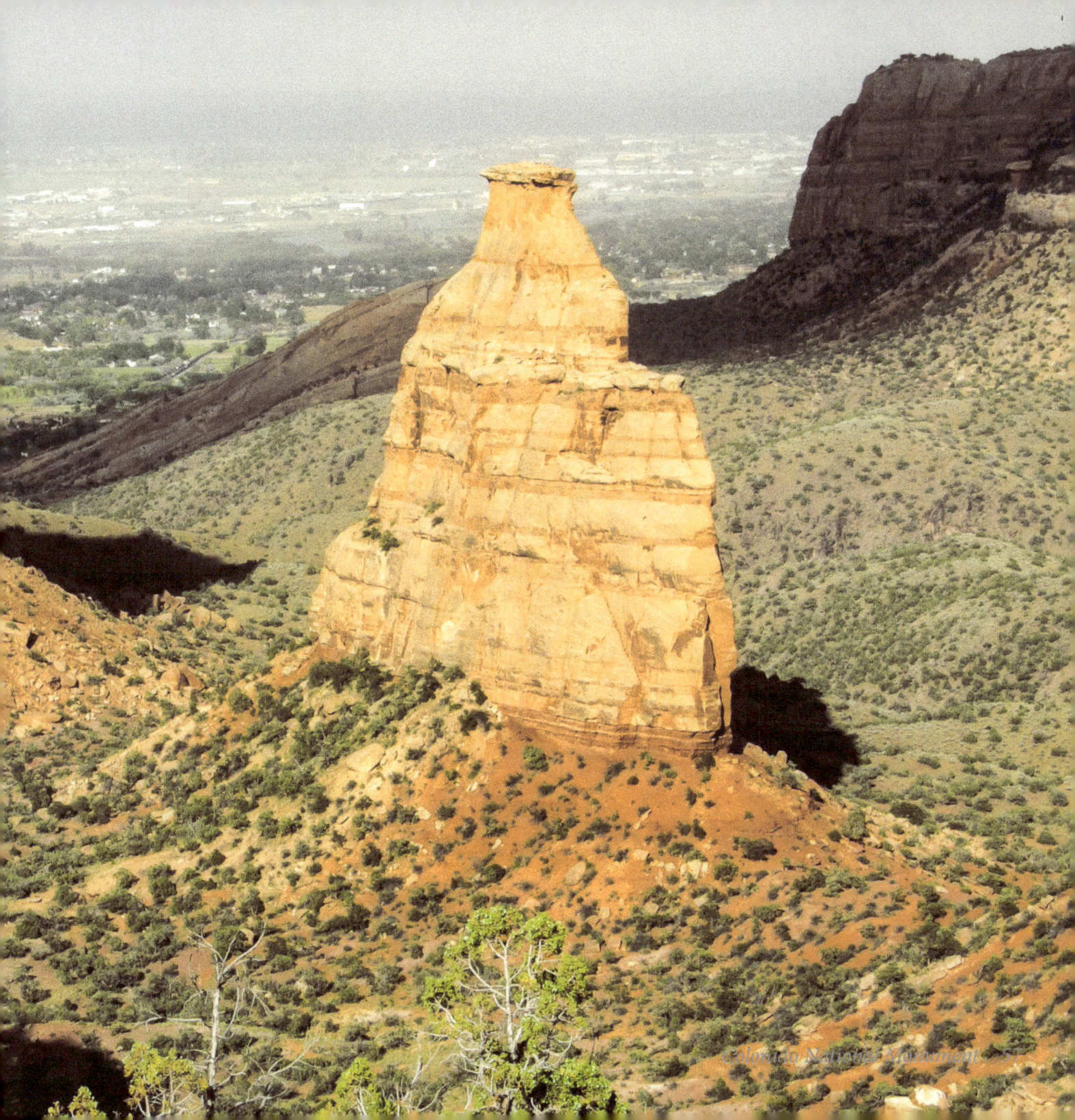

Colorado National Monument

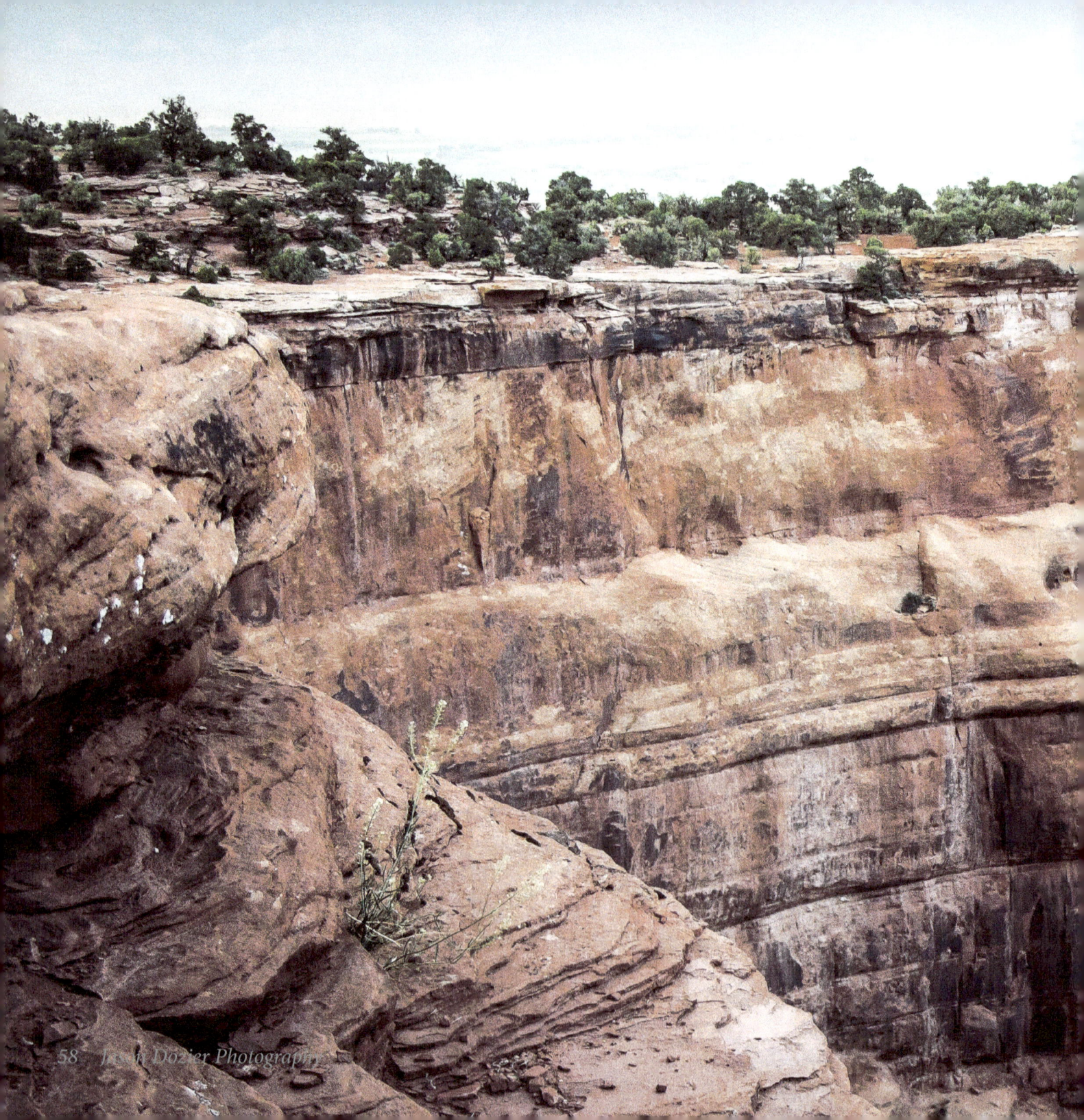

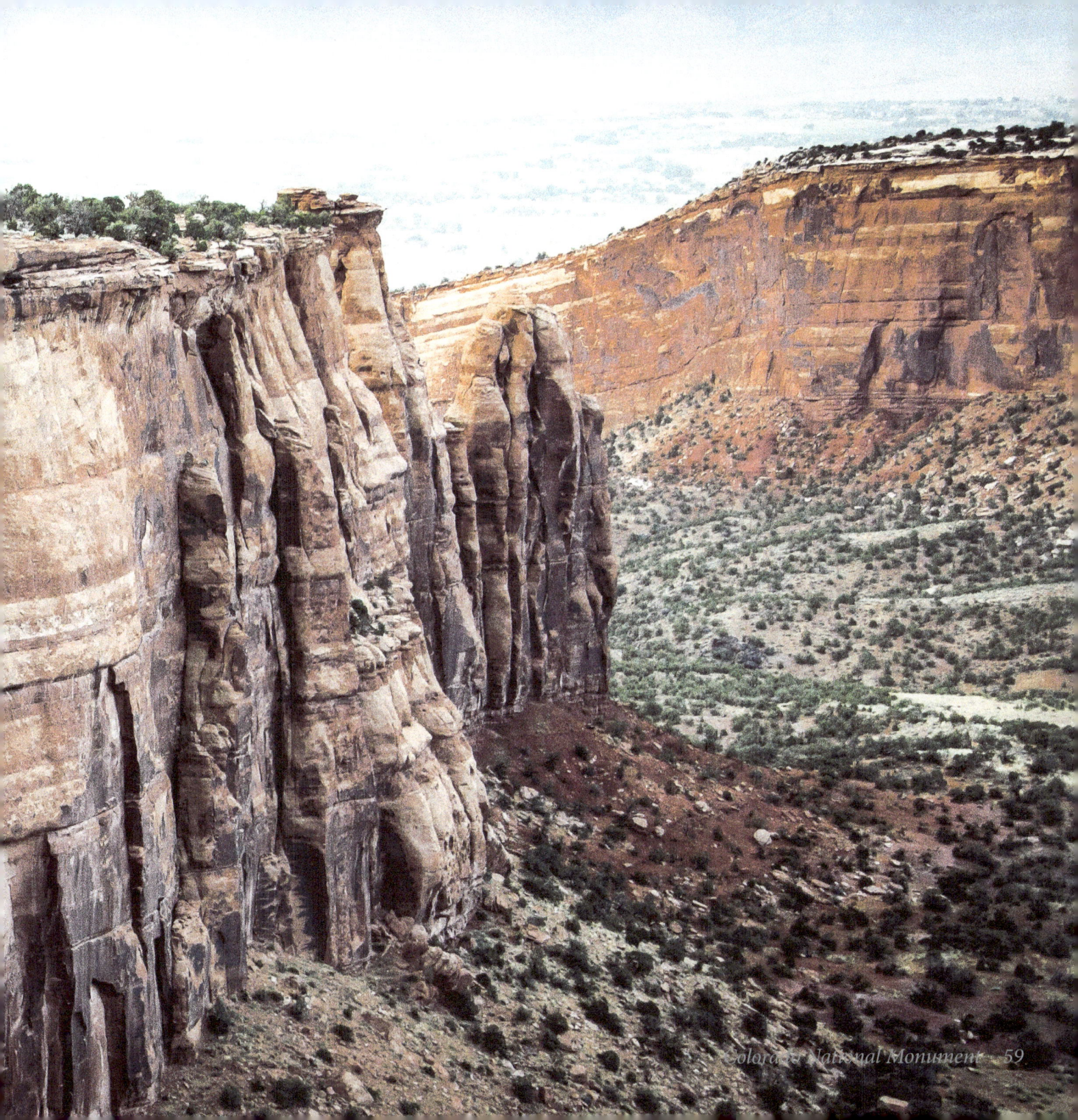

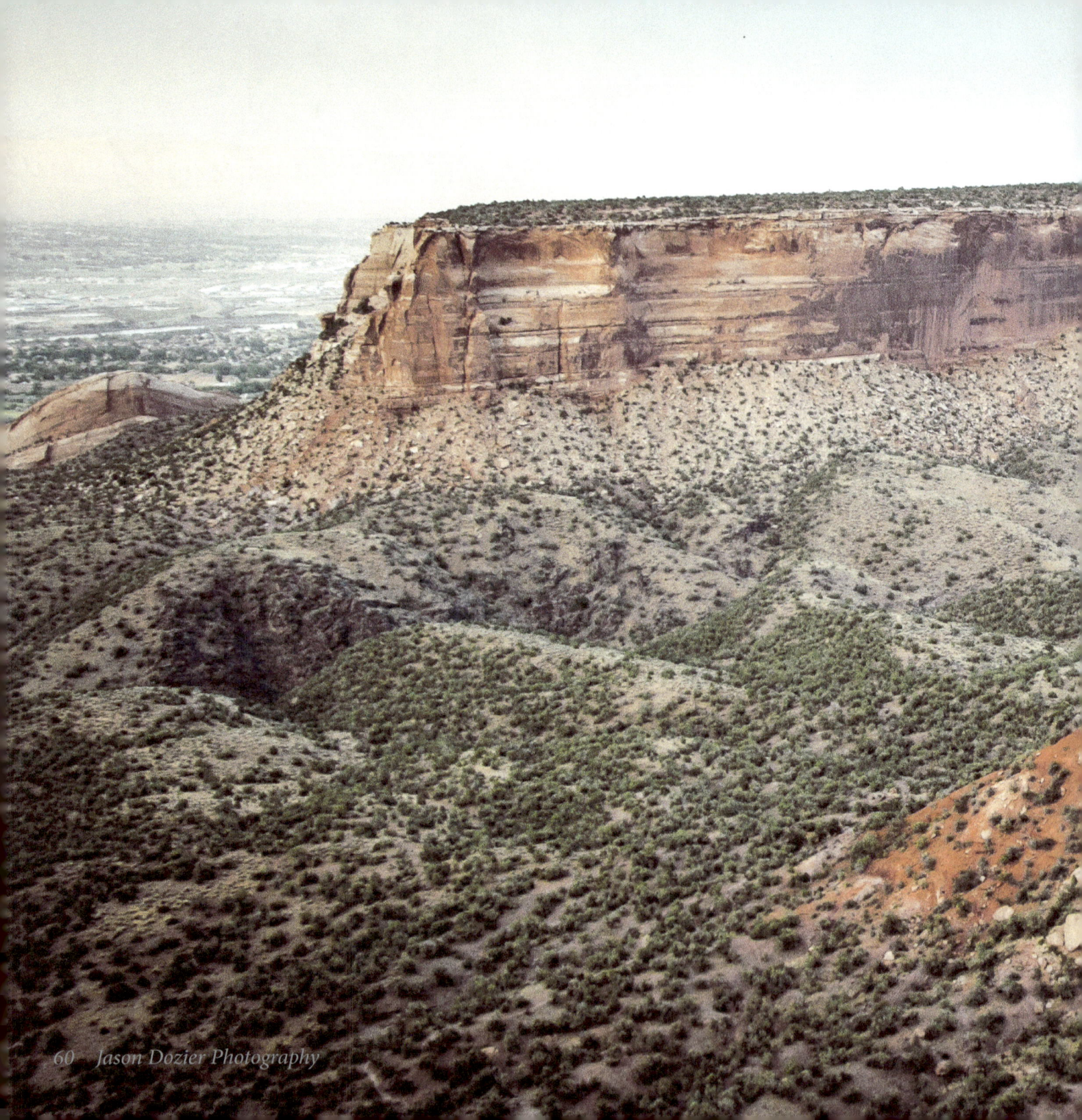

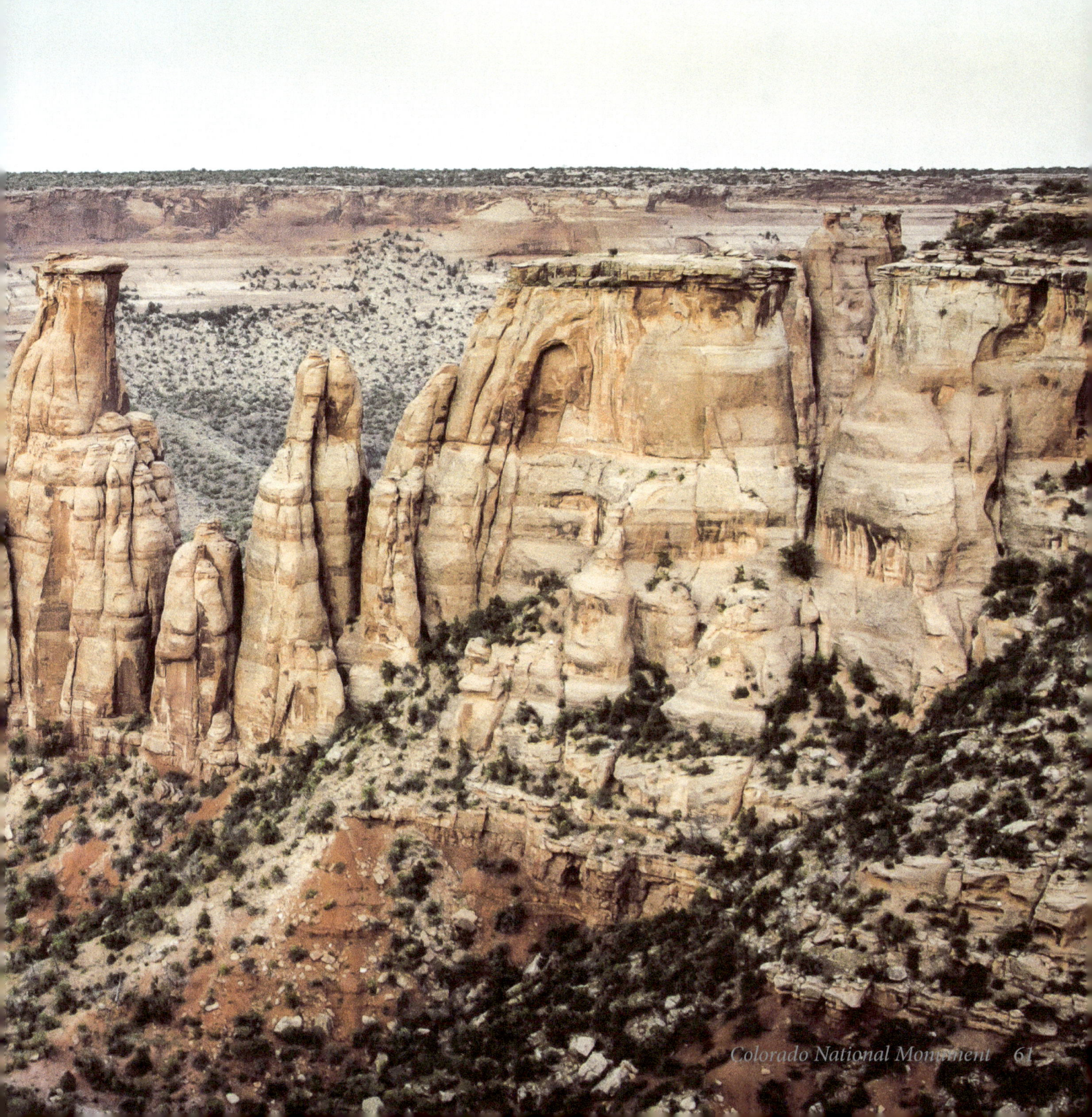

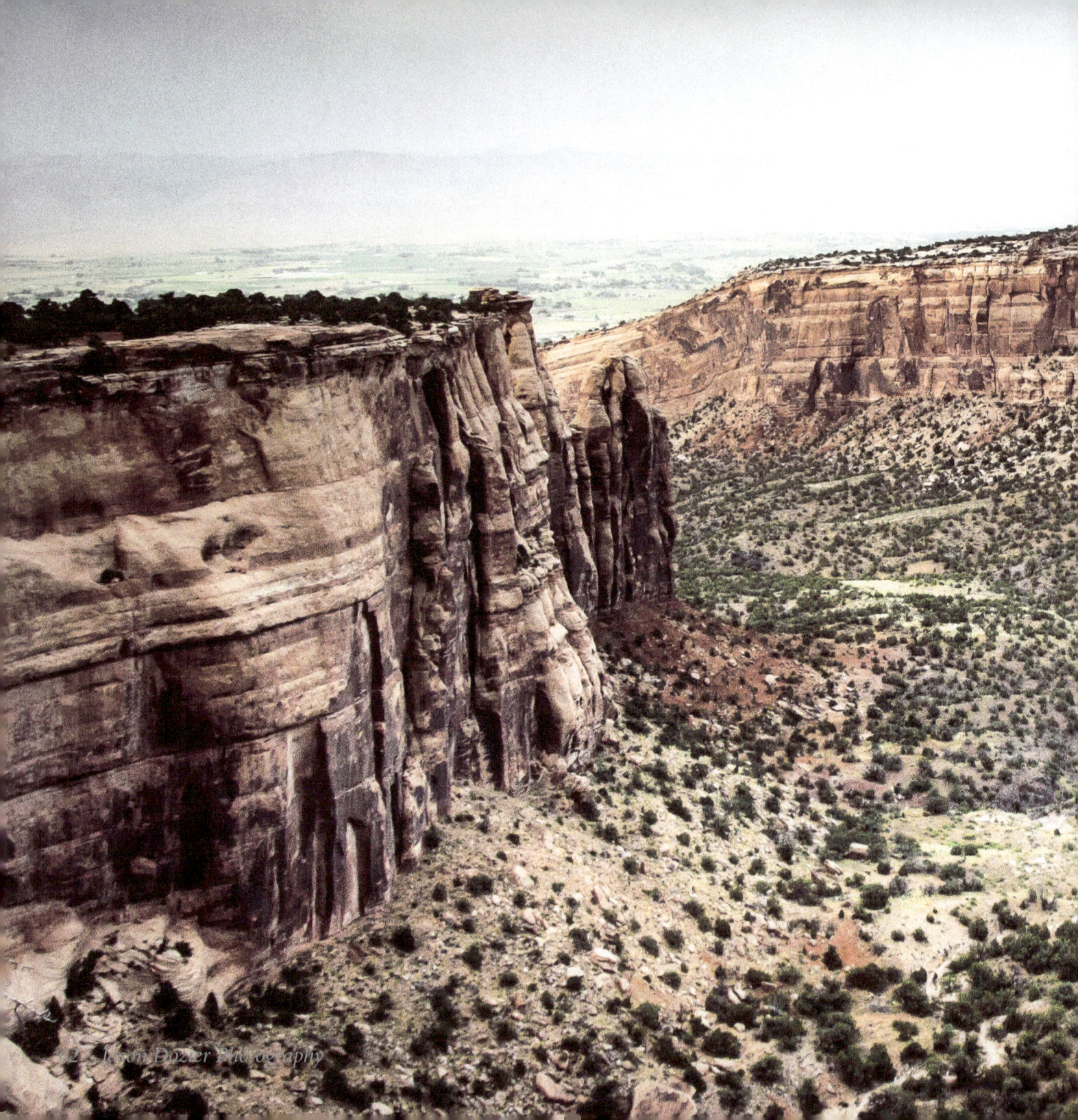

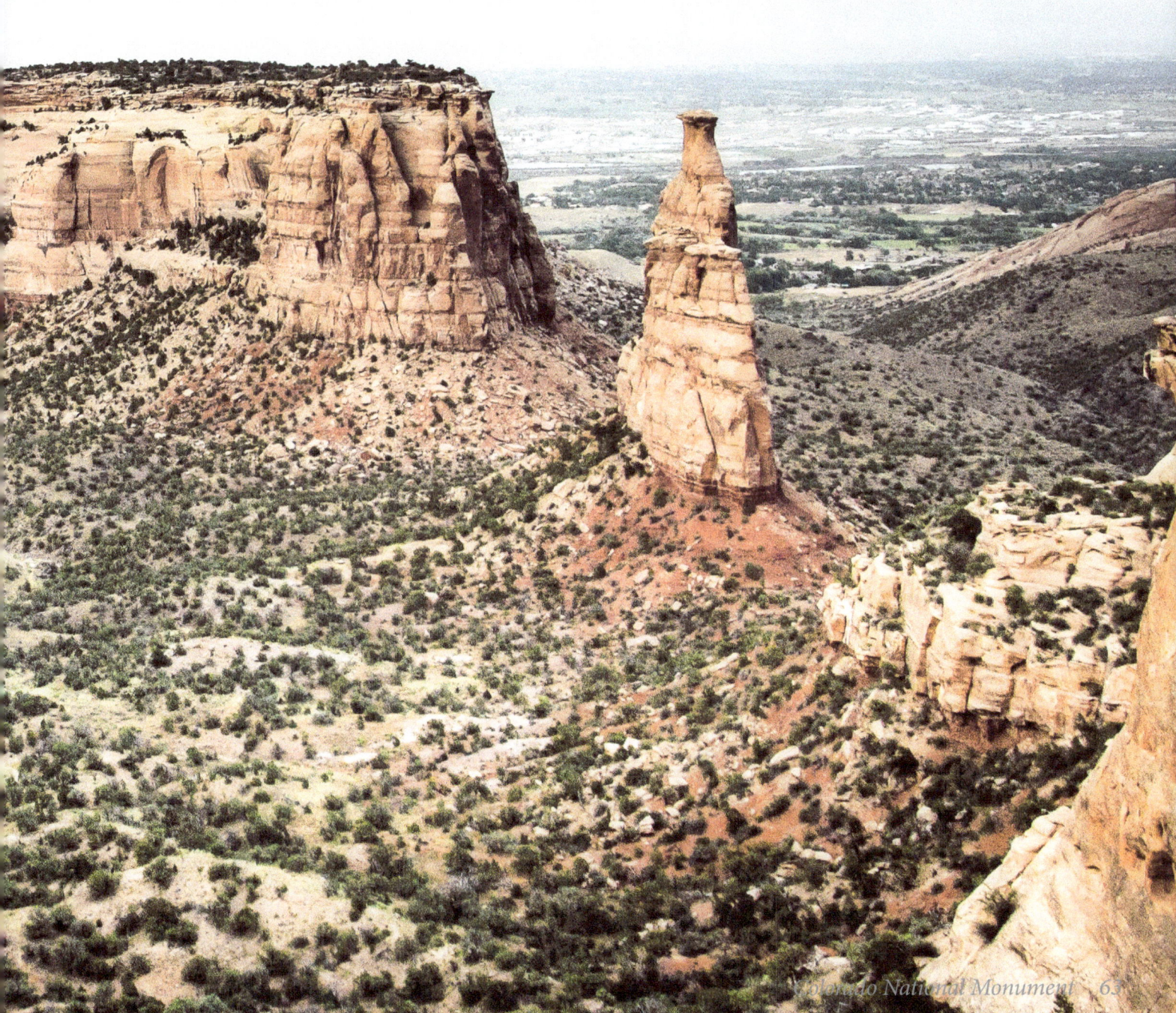

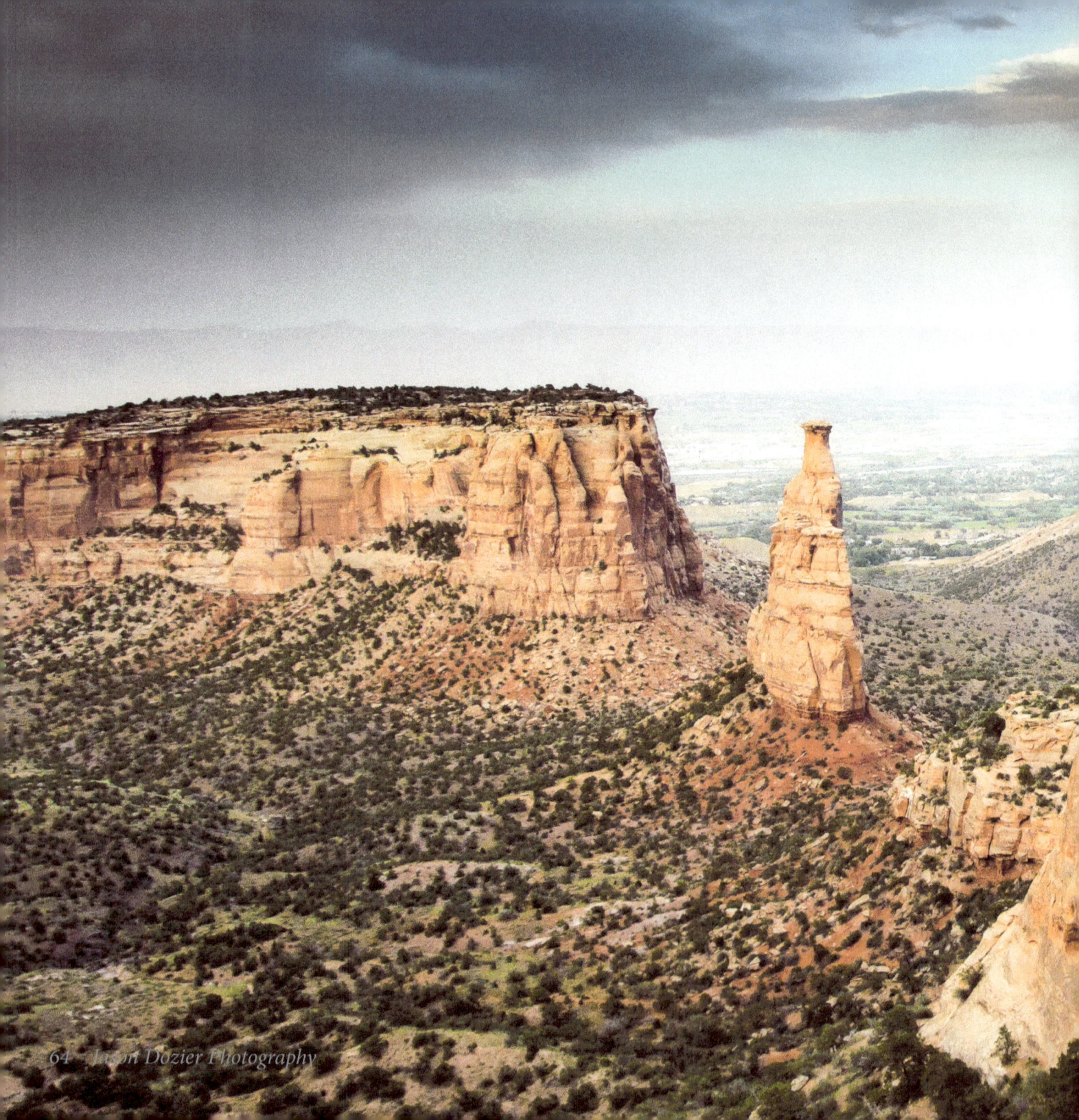

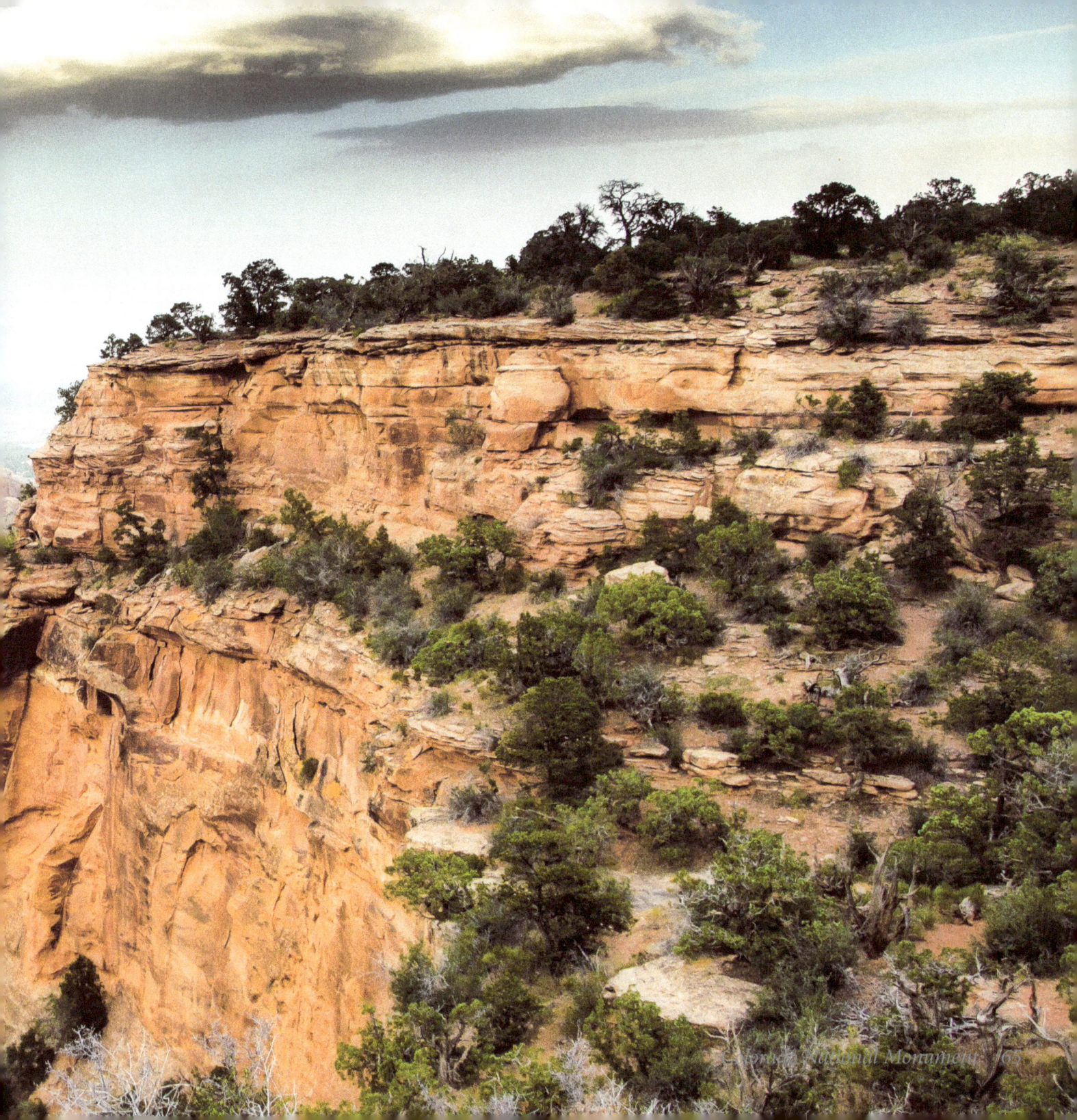

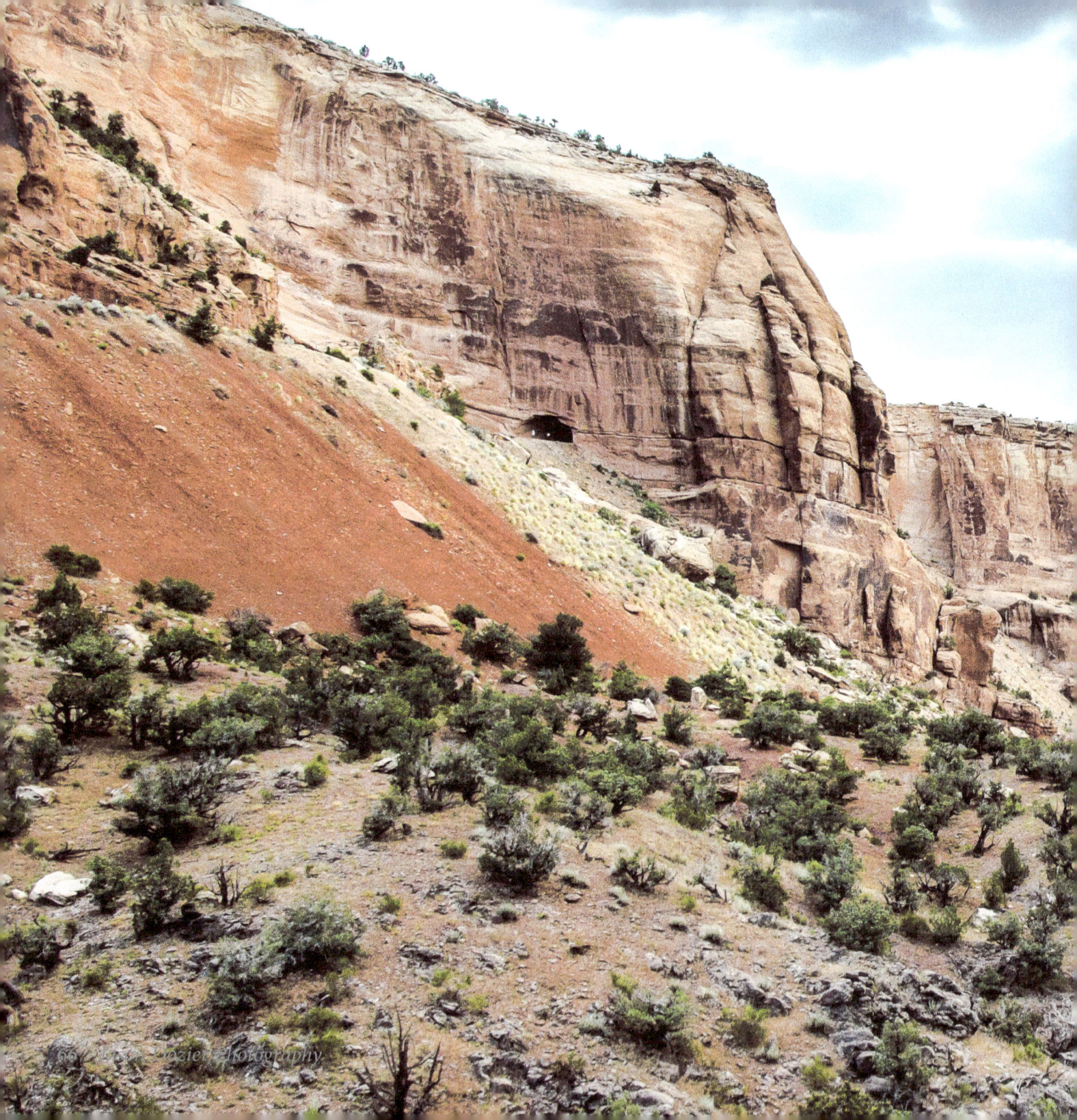

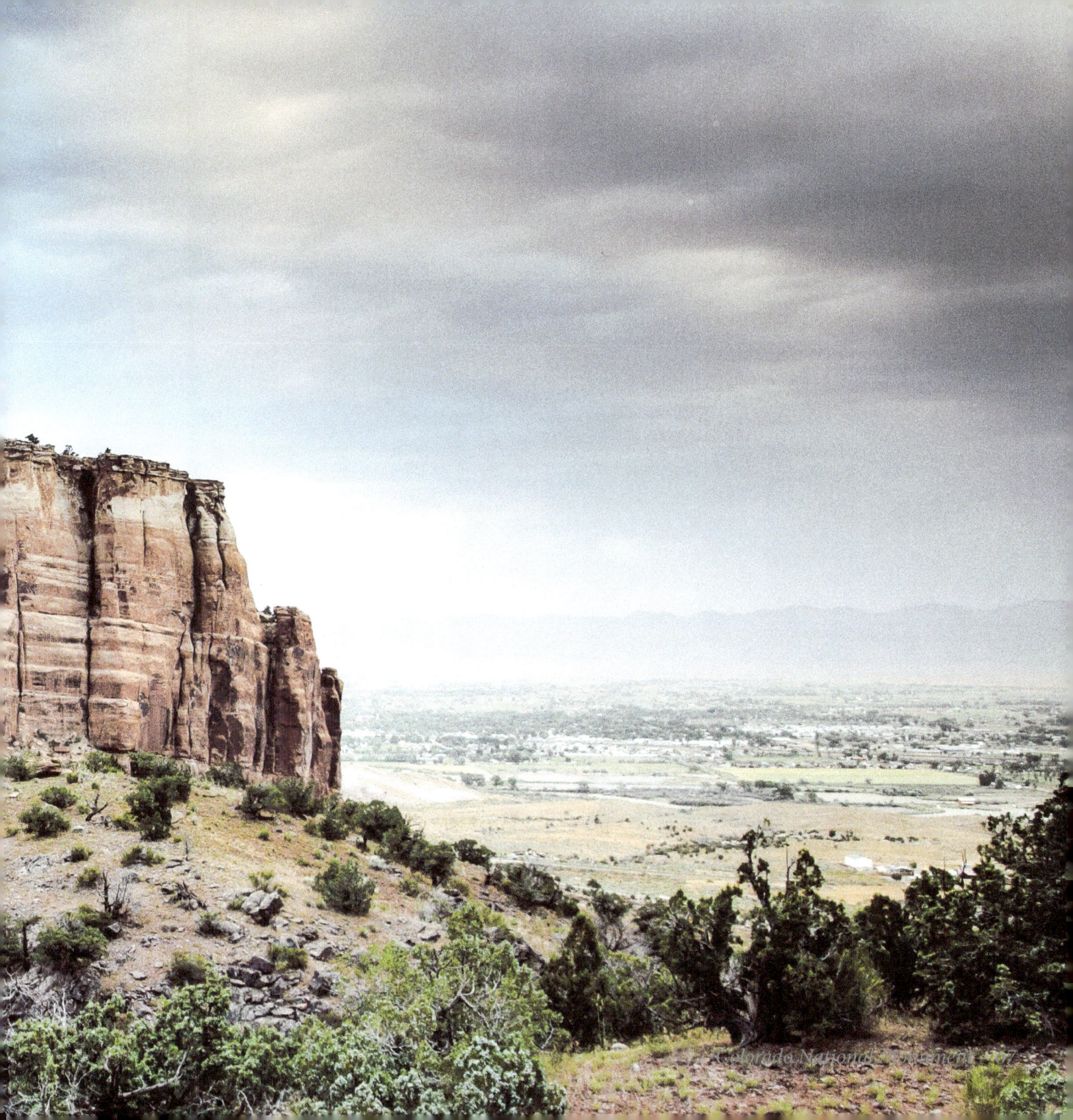

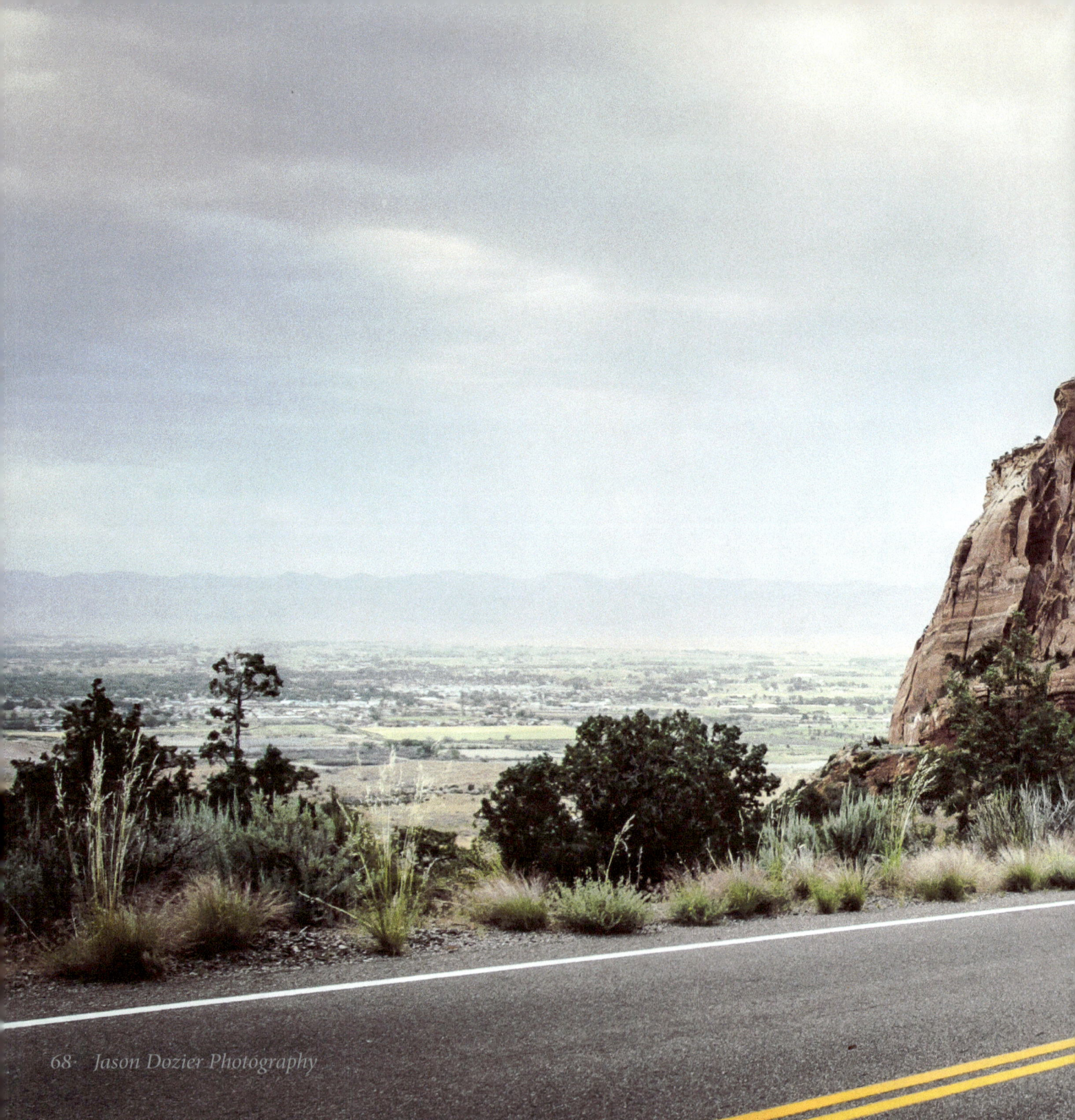

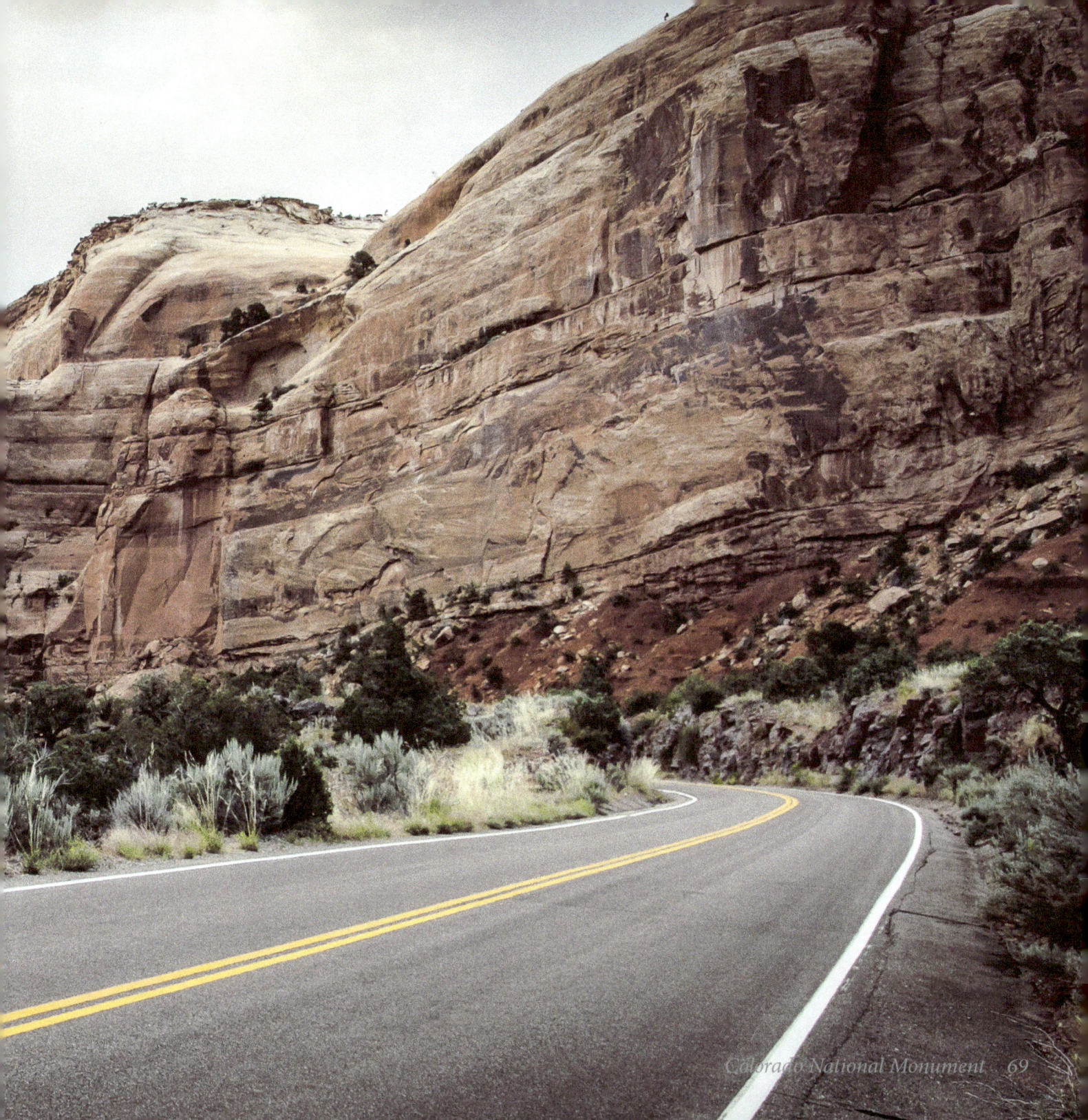

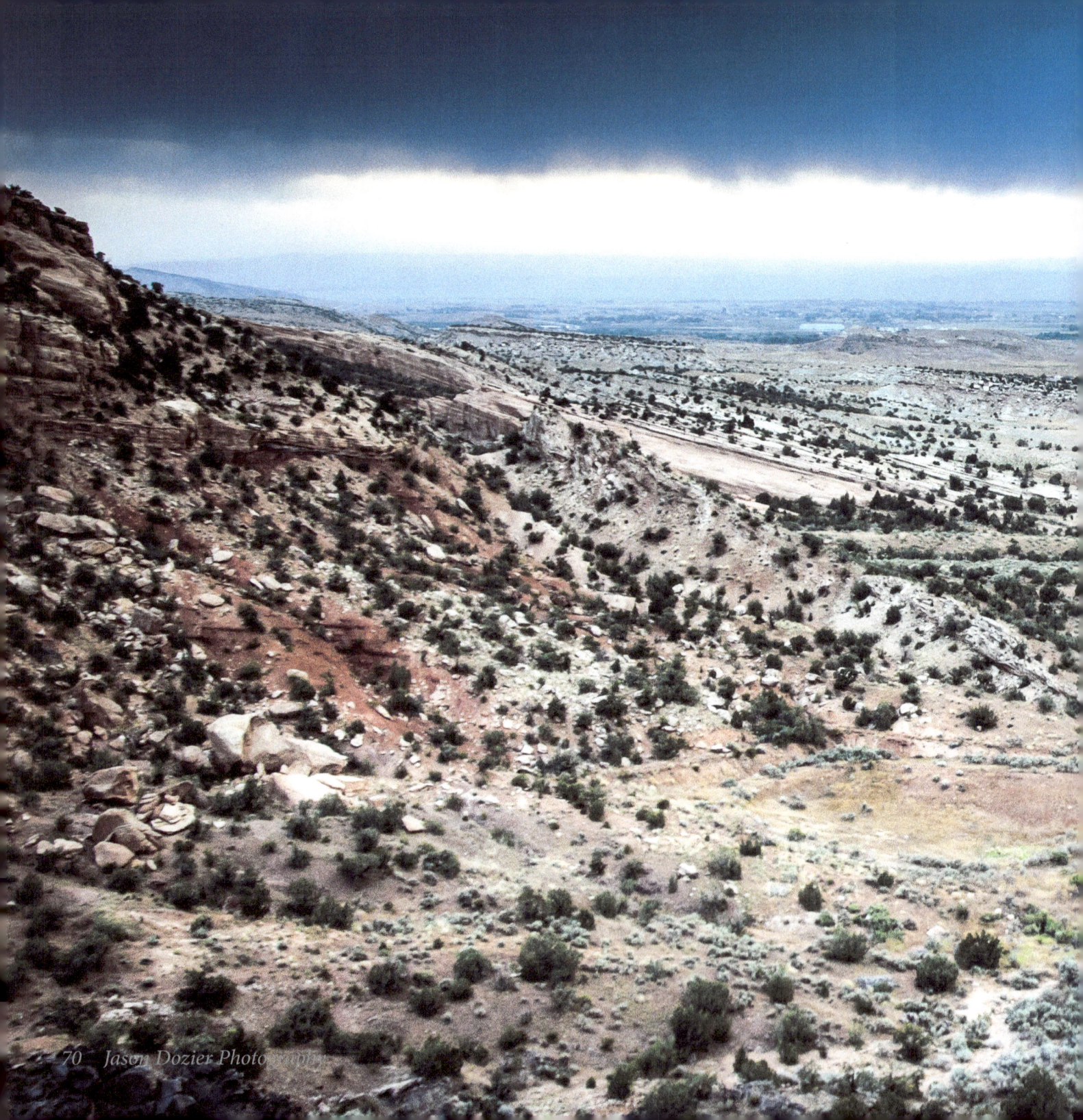

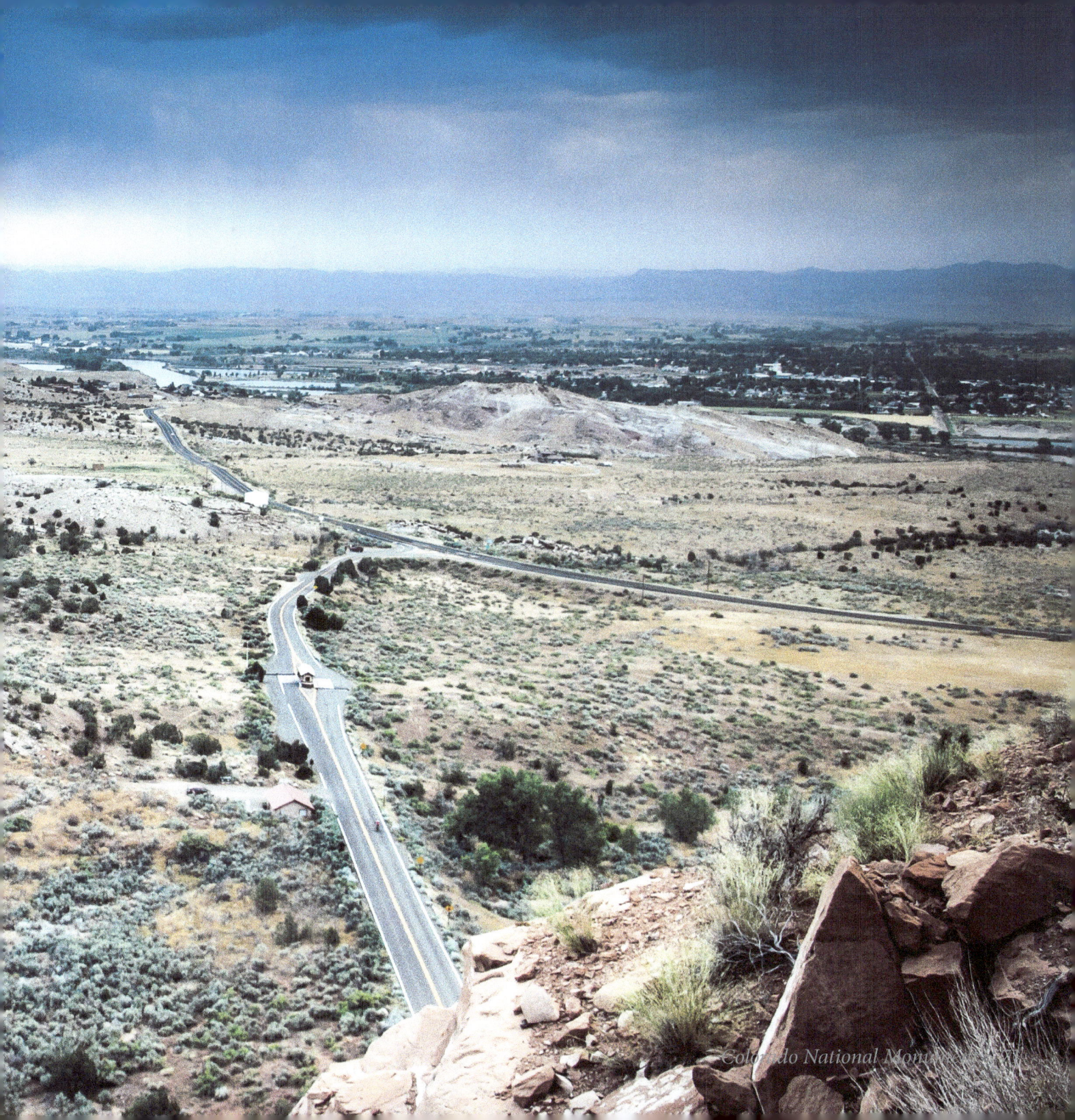

Colorado National Monument

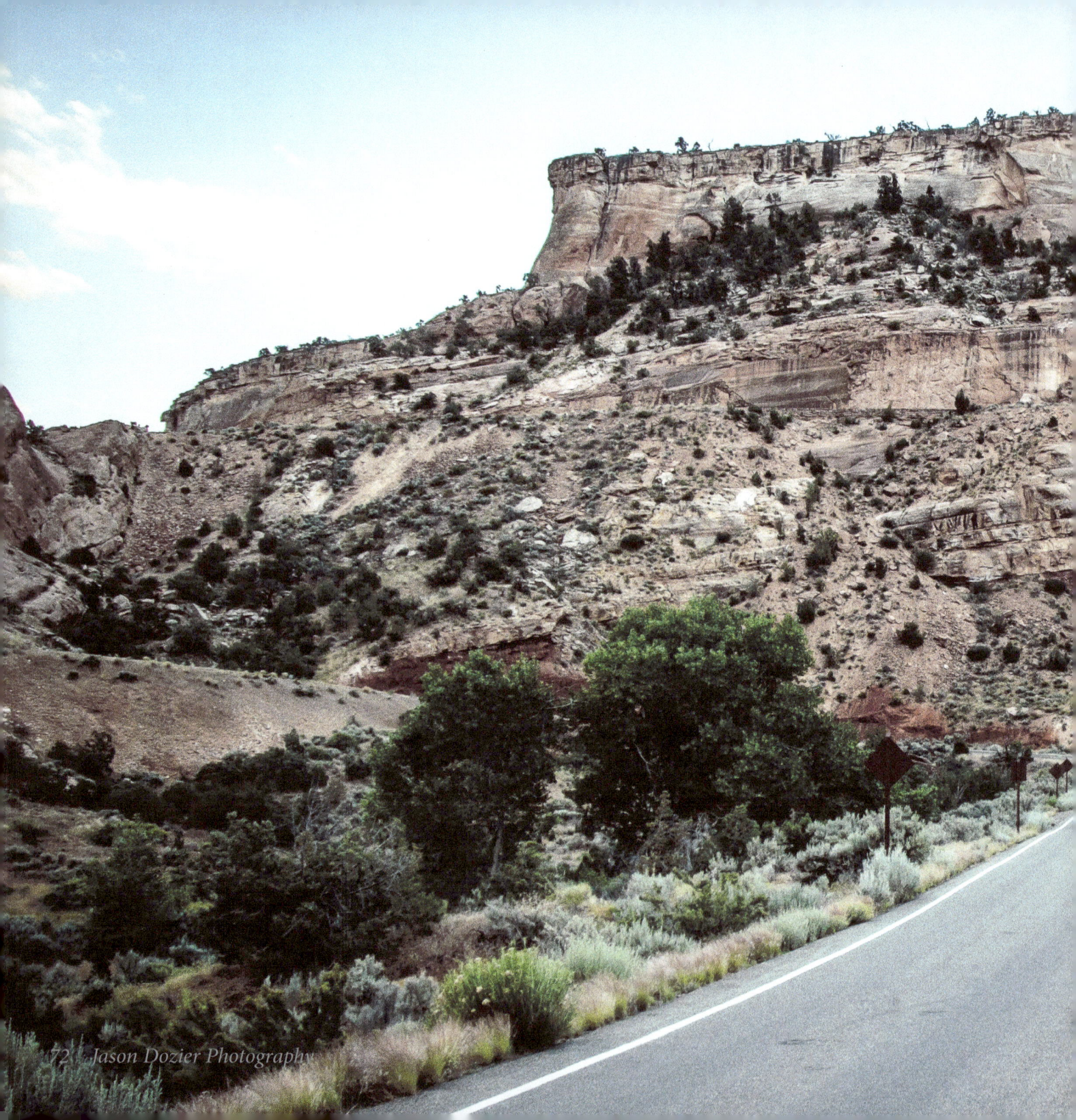

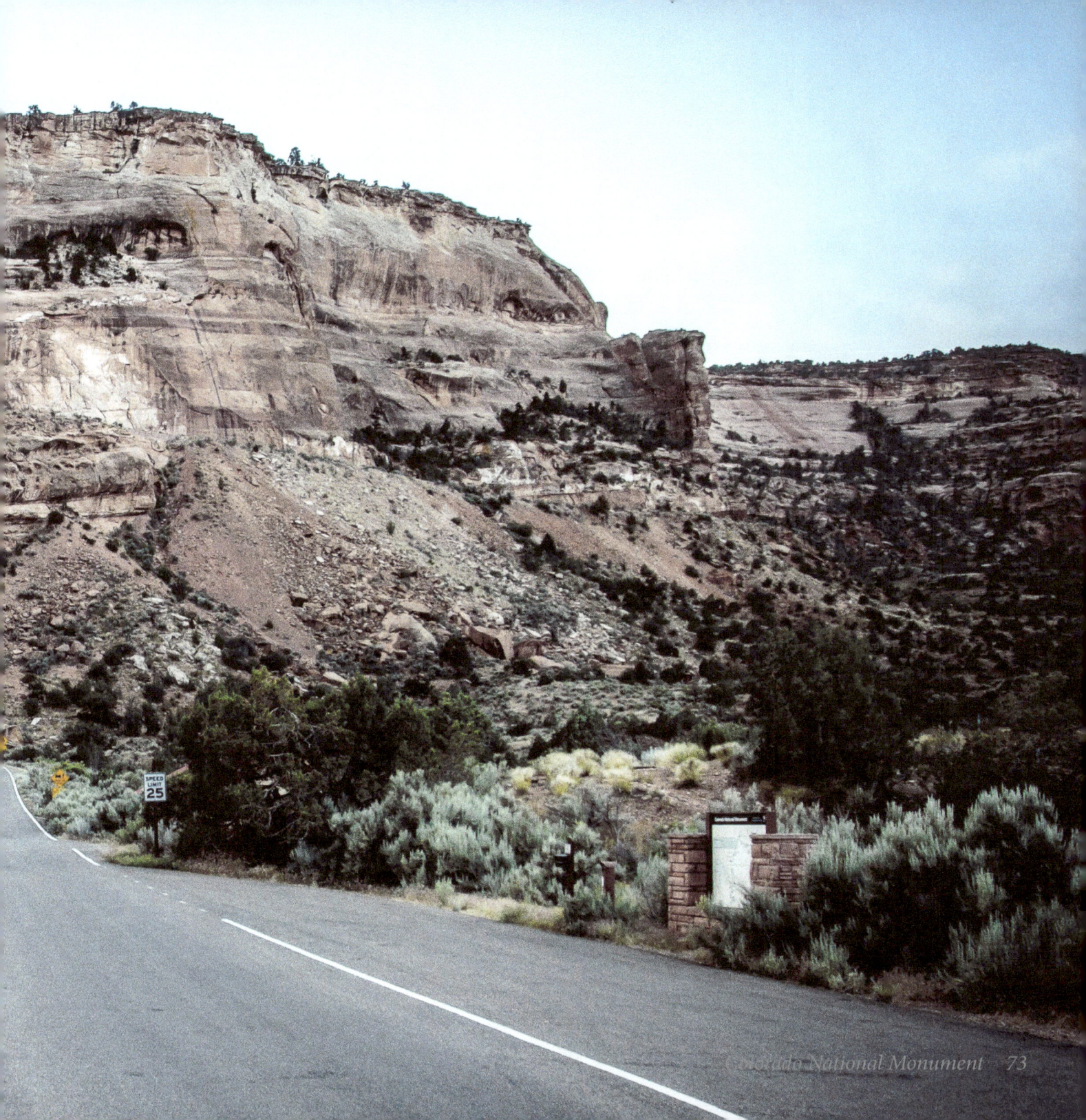

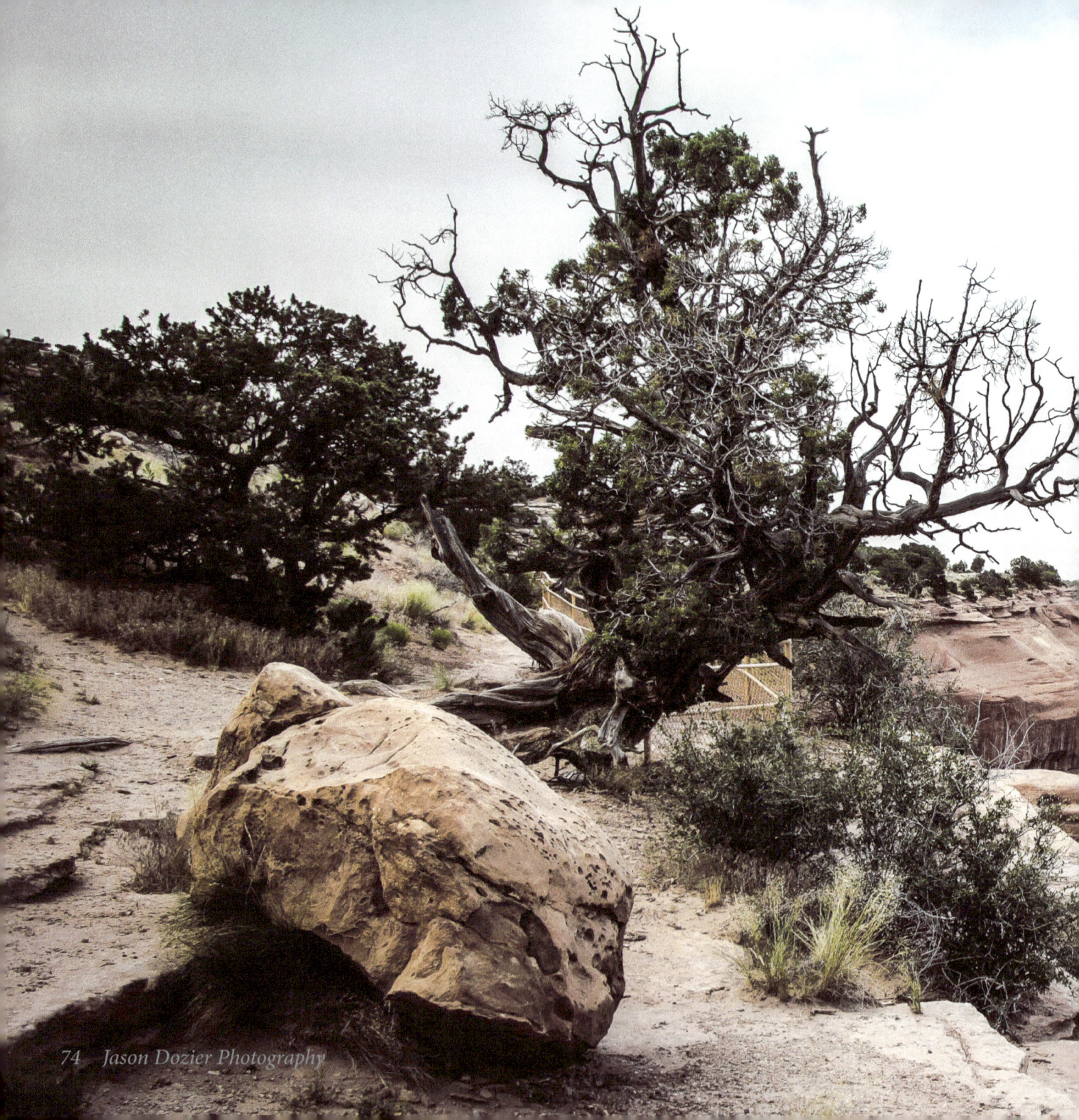

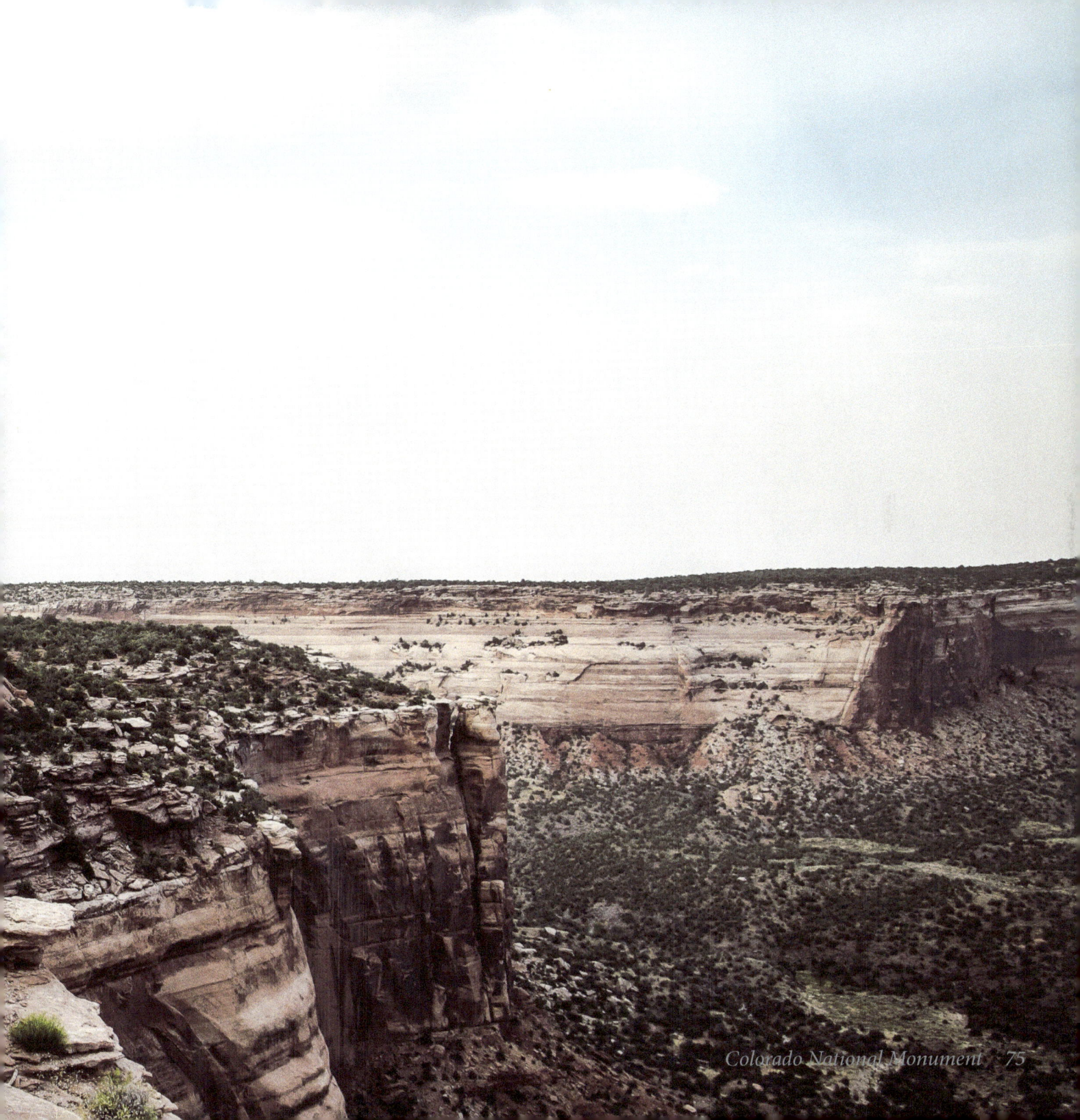

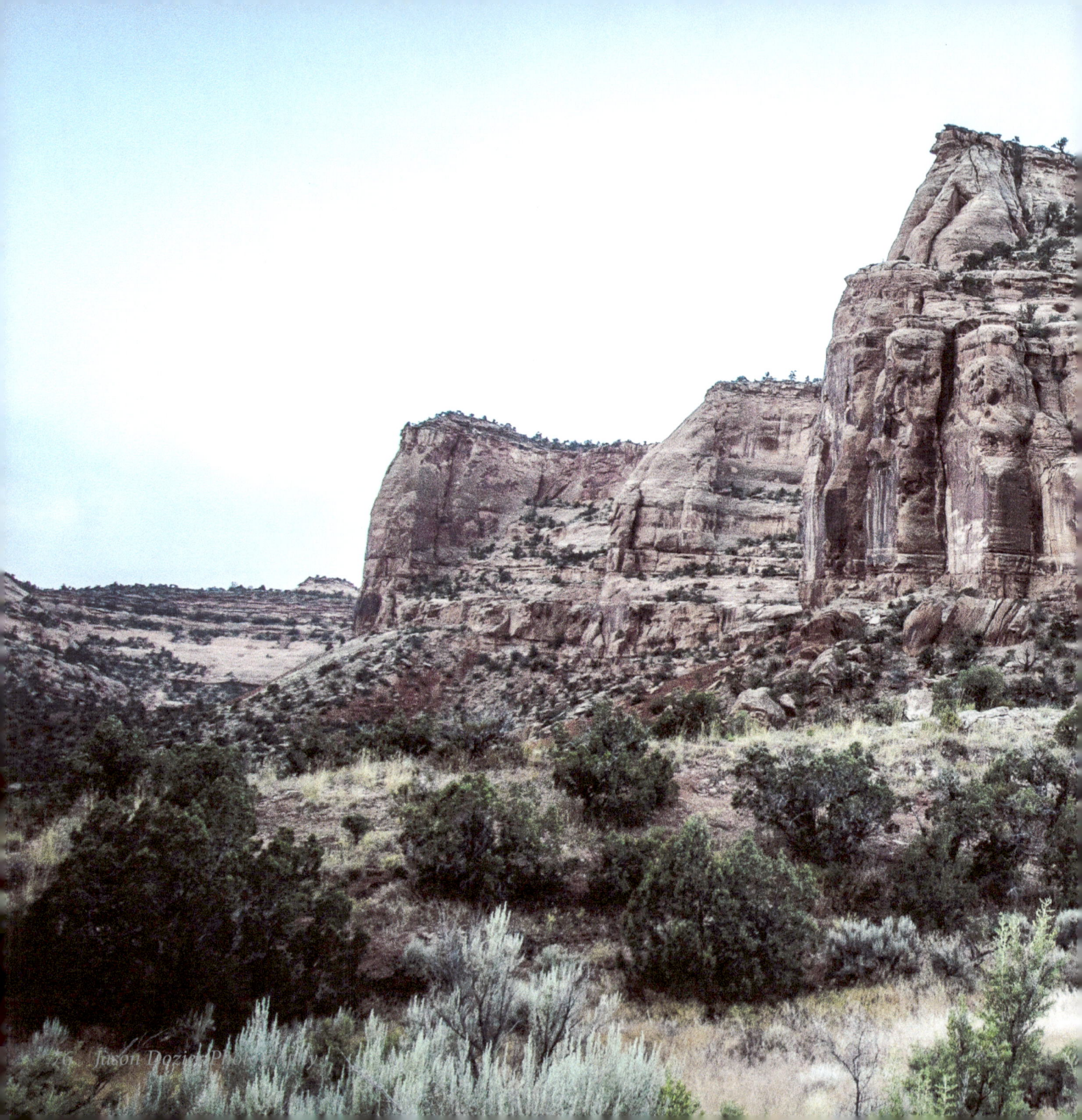

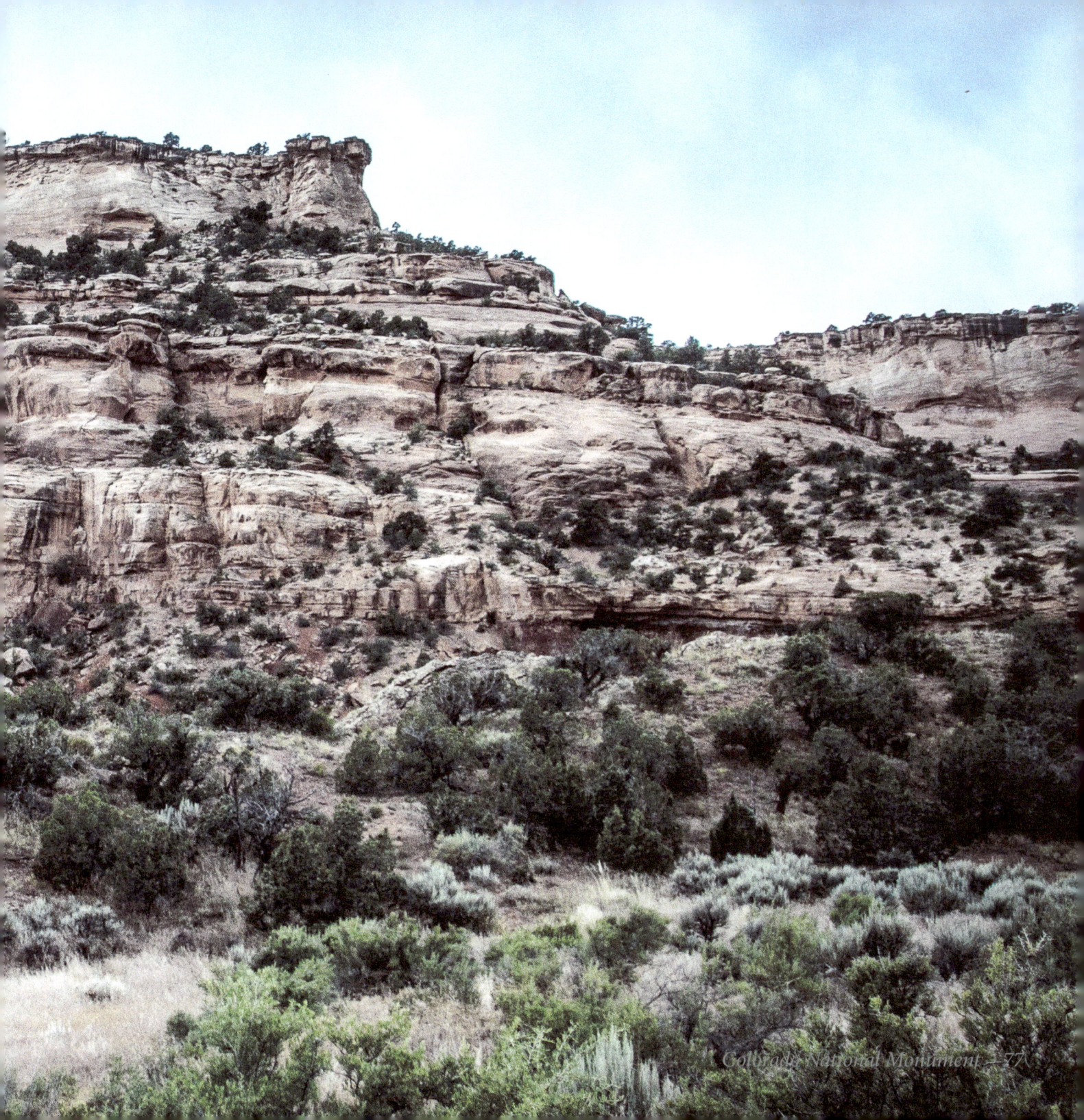

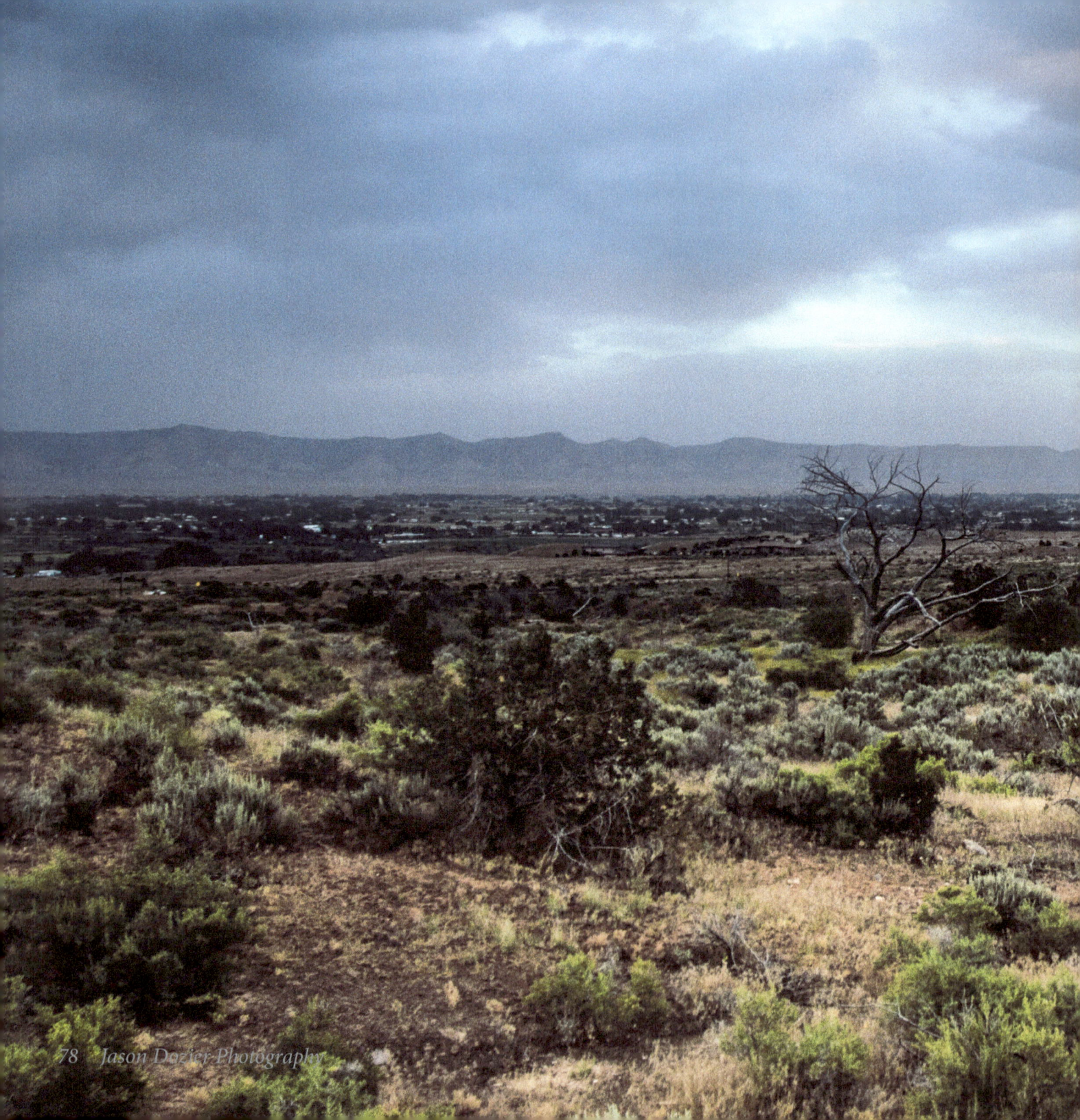

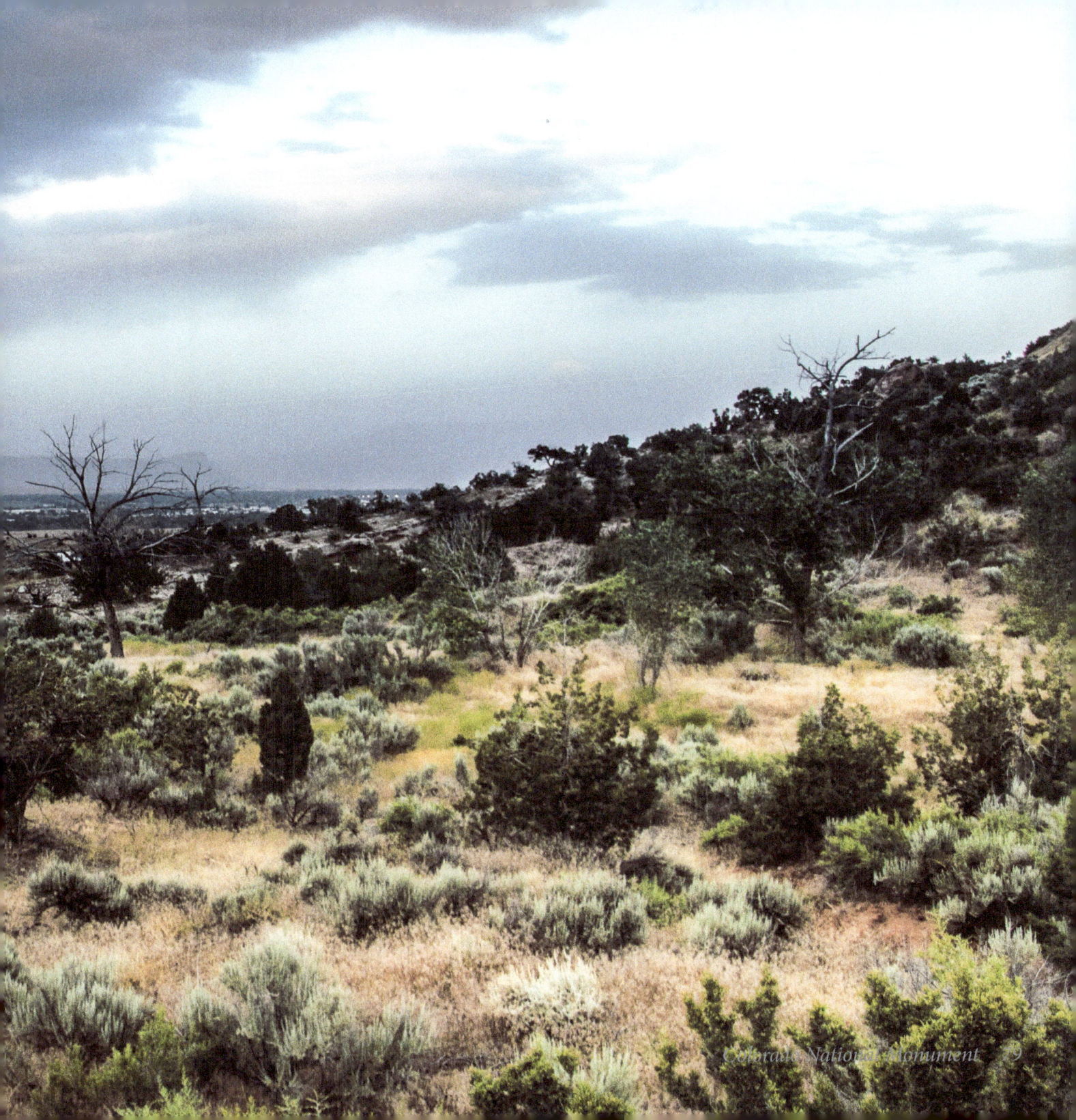

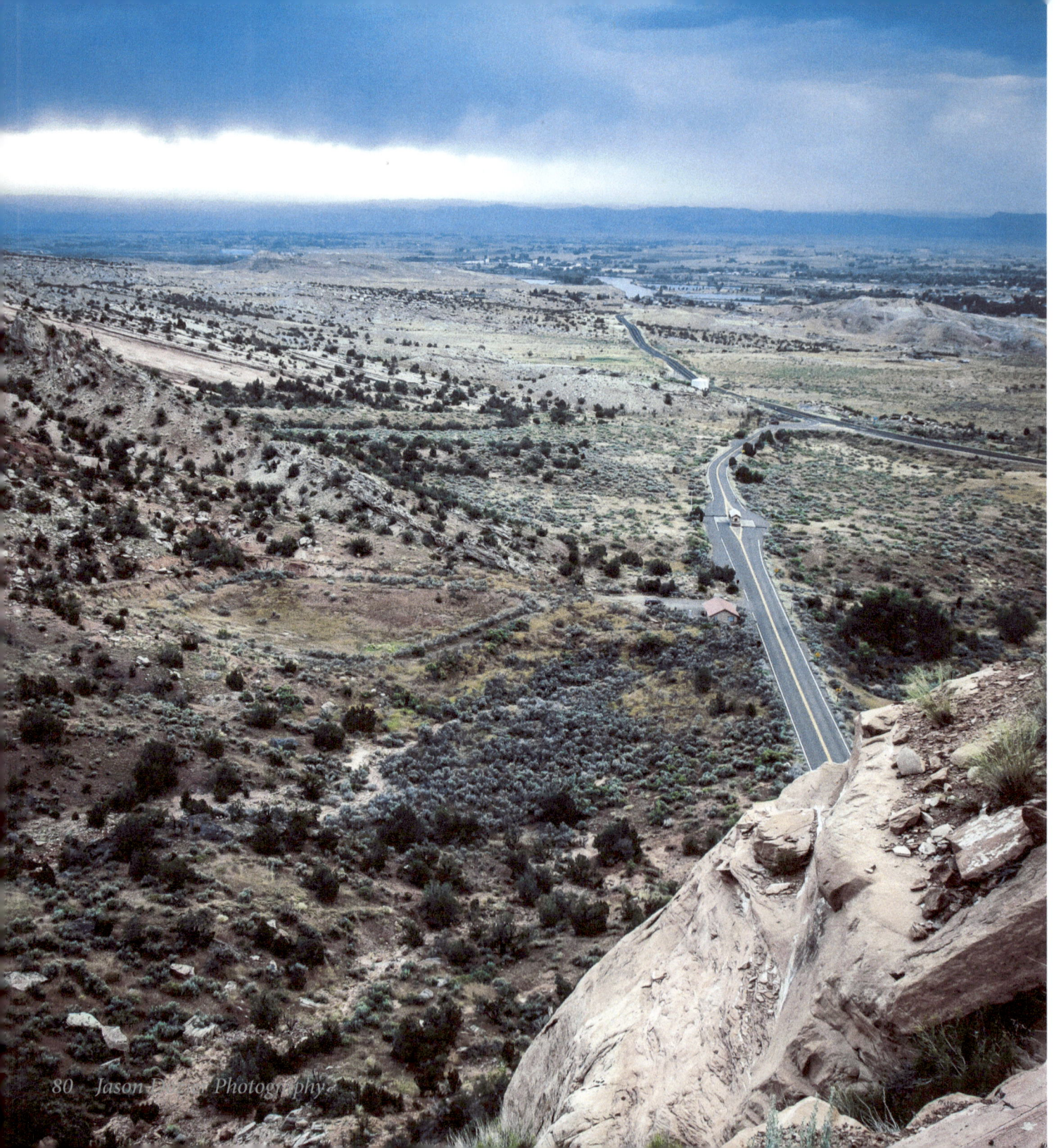